Ruffing It

The Complete Guide to Camping with Dogs

Mardi Richmond
and
Melanee L. Barash

Alpine
PUBLICATIONS
Loveland, CO

RUFFING IT: THE COMPLETE GUIDE TO CAMPING WITH DOGS

Library of Congress Cataloging-in-Publication Data

Richmond, Mardi, 1960-
    Ruffing it: the complete guide to camping with dogs / Mardi Richmond and Melanee L. Barash.
        p. cm.
    Includes bibliographical references and index.
    ISBN 1-57779-009-X (softcover)
    1. Camping with dogs. I. Barash, Melanee L., 1956-
II. Title.
    SF427.455.R535 1998
796.54—dc21   98-36665
                                                     CIP

Many manufacturers secure trademark rights for their products. When Alpine Publications is aware of a trademark claim, we identify the product name by using initial capital letters.

For the sake of simplicity, the terms "he" or "she" are sometimes used to identify an animal or person. These are used in the generic sense only. No discrimination of any kind is intended toward either sex.

Alpine Publications accepts no responsibility for medical information, suggested treatments, or vaccinations mentioned herein. The reader is advised to check with their local, licensed veterinarian before giving medical attention.

This book is available at special quantity discounts for breeders and for club promotions, premiums, or educational use. Write for details.

Cover Photo: "Minnie," courtesy Mary Kroske and Jean Fairbanks
Text photos by: Mardi Richmond and Melanee L. Barash, except where otherwise noted
Illustrations by: Mardi Richmond
Edited by: Dianne Nelson
Design and layout by: Shadow Canyon Graphics

First printing 1998
1 2 3 4 5 6 7 8 9 0

Printed in the United States of America

CONTENTS

Dedicated to Charlie and Dakota,
our original trailblazers,
and to canine campers everywhere.
Wishing you many happy adventures.

ACKNOWLEDGMENTS

We would like to thank all of the beings, two- and four-legged, who helped with the creation of this book. We could not have done it without your assistance, support, kindness, and tail-wagging encouragement. Thank you to:

Jeffrey Grudin, DVM; Kerrin Hoban, DVM; Hannah Good, DVM; Cally Haber, LAC, Kendall, and Chako; Penny and Mike Brozda and Mattie; Kathy Kern, AHT, and her ever-growing pack; Mary Kroske, Jean Fairbanks, Minnie, and Lily; Tom Davis and Hueco; Shoshana Coplan, Leslie Smith, Raphael, Brindie, and Runi; Hilary Farberow, Gary Steven Stuart, Gucci Lucille, and Rainier; Sharon Heckert, David Farberow, Luna, and Sam; Melissa Orlie, Jasper, and Horton; Jennifer Holz, Yar, and Sasha; Kat Brown and "A Kitty Dog"; Angela Glass, Lisa Jensen, B.J., Ozzie, Suki, Charley, and Harley; Joyce Rowland, Ollie, Max, and Drifter; Judith, Russell, Isabel Carey, and Leo; Val Leoffler; Michael and Anita Mezey and Pee Dee of Pee Dee's Paw Protectors; Pam Paulson of Dog Days of Wisconsin; Wendy Ballard of *DogGone Newsletter*; Darren L. Smith of *Parks Directory of the U.S.*; Charlie, Dakota, Moose, Cowboy, Blue, Jesse, and, of course, Sam. There are many other beings, human, canine, and more, too numerous to mention separately, that have helped us along the way. Please know that you have our sincerest gratitude and wishes for many happy trails.

Special thanks to Kita Glass for his suggestions, encouragement, and incredible patience.

Camping with your dog makes the trip ten times as much fun.
PHOTO COURTESY PENNY AND MIKE BROZDA

WHY CAMPING?

A re you an avid camper with a new canine friend? Or a new camper wanting to share good times with your dog? Have you and your dog already shared many outdoor adventures? Then this book is for you, whether you are brand new to the experience or planning your fiftieth trip.

Dogs on Vacation

Camping with dogs can be an ideal vacation for many reasons, not the least of which is the expense—or lack thereof. Camping is a downright cheap way to get away from the challenges of everyday life. You'll be on vacation, but you can leave your credit card at home. No boarding kennels for your canine friend and no kennel or pet-sitting charges for you. And you don't have to worry about "ruffing it" being too rough! You can make camping suit your comfort level—from the wildest back-country adventure to the tamest creature comfort campground.

Camping can also be a great way to travel, get away from your hectic schedules and see new places. One friend described the differences between camping and staying in a motel this way: "In a motel," she said, "you see the beach out your window—maybe even take a walk before dinner or a swim after lunch. But with camping, you'll not only see the ocean out the window of your tent, you'll also hear it lulling you to sleep and wake up to its fresh, salty smell. Your senses come alive. You get to experience the place you're visiting in all of its complexities and layers."

Camping with your dog means sharing the adventure and fun with your best friend. You'll get to walk together, sleep together, and eat together. You and your dog will get to know each other in new ways. Camping with your dog will help you see the world through different eyes—your dog's. Dogs experience the world differently than people. They are more aware and alert. They sense the rabbit with their ears and nose before human eyes pick up the sight. When your dog's ears go up, you know that something is moving nearby. When he raises his nose to the wind, you know that an enticing smell is on the horizon (it may simply be another camper's dinner, or it could be that coyote you were hoping to catch sight of).

Dogs keep you aware—and they also keep you active. They like to move and explore. Their curiosity takes you to places you might not go alone. Take a few moments now to visualize the experience. Imagine walking down a trail with your dog at your heel. Think about sitting in front of a campfire with your dog's head resting on your knee. Picture your dog snuggled in your tent, keeping your feet warm on a cold, crisp night. It is an experience you will never forget.

Canine Curiosity

Of course, a dog's curiosity can also take you places you wish you'd never even thought about. Consider what would happen if you and your dog met up with a skunk on the trail. Sleeping together in a tent that night might not be such a warm or wonderful experience.

Camping with a dog has its risks. What if your dog takes off down a ravine and corners a rattlesnake? What if your dog catches up with a raccoon? And, of course, your dog poses a serious risk to those same wild animals.

Dogs are a mixture of warm and loving pack animals and instinctive hunters. Some dogs have prey drives that liken them to their wild brothers and sisters—wolves, coyotes, and foxes. Others, whose hunting sides have been bred out of them, might still enjoy a romp after a rabbit just for fun. But your dog's fun could put the other animal in danger.

You also need to consider problems like giardia—that common parasite found in the rivers and streams of the United States. And how will your dog get along with other dogs and campers? What about the dog that gets too sore or tired to have any fun, much less make the long trek back to the car or campsite? How about those soft city paws? How do you prevent bleeding pads?

You get the picture.

With all of these potential pitfalls, is camping really such a great idea? If you haven't tried it yet, you may be wondering why you'd embark on such an adventure. But with a little know-how and planning, every one of those potential problems (and many more) can be avoided. If you have camped with your dog, you already know that there is nothing quite like it. Camping is fun, relaxing, and freeing.

And that's why we wrote this book—to help you be prepared and have fun!

A Note About Leashes

As you flip through this book, you will see pictures of dogs on leash and off leash. For some of you, the off-leash dog may seem the happiest. Others may be concerned at seeing an off-leash dog. Both are valid points of view. There is nothing more beautiful than watching your dog take off through a meadow or head full speed down a beach, running out all that energy. There is also nothing more aggravating and unsafe than having an off-leash dog that is not under voice control (meaning he will *always* come when called). Worse yet, a dog off leash where it is illegal poses the risk of losing access for even leashed dogs in the future. Our guidelines for leash use are:

1. Only let your dog off leash if he is under good voice control, meaning that he will come back immediately when called *under any circumstance*. This is important for the safety of the wildlife *and* your dog.

2. Even well-trained dogs are tempted by hopping rabbits or other wildlife. If you have any doubt about your dog's response, use a long leash instead of no leash. Your dog can run, romp, and explore with you still in control.

3. *Never* let a dog off leash where there are rules or laws prohibiting it—even if the dog is under good voice control. If you do, you risk losing access for dogs to all camping areas. You may also be cited or fined.

CHAPTER ONE

CHOOSING THE RIGHT
TYPE OF CAMPING

Car camping, backpacking, RV camping, canoeing, bicycle touring—there are enough types of camping to fit any temperament and lifestyle. All can be great fun with a dog, depending, of course, on your expectations and level of preparation.

Hilary, for example, loves camping with her dog Gucci. She and her family will head out on the weekends in their van, find a nice spot, and enjoy getting away from it all. They are comfortable camping together and generally have a great time. Hilary knows how Gucci will respond in the wilderness. She knows what will get Gucci excited and what will calm her down, and she's learned how to prepare for a trip with her dog. But she learned some of it the hard way on her first backpacking trip with Gucci.

Hilary, an experienced backpacker, thought that her new dog Gucci would take immediately to the trail. Gucci, a big, athletic dog, loved to romp—perfect for backpacking. When Hilary, Gucci, and their camping companions reached the trailhead in the Sisters Wilderness Area in Oregon, Hilary pulled out the dog backpack that she had brought for Gucci. She proceeded to fill it with brown paper bags full of dog food and fit it to Gucci's back. As Hilary fastened the belts around Gucci's chest and belly, Gucci stood patiently. But as soon as Hilary released Gucci, the dog took off, frantically running up and down the trail, rubbing against trees, rolling on the ground, shaking the pack, pulling at the pack—all in an attempt to get the confounded pack off her back.

After almost an hour of these antics—with Hilary alternately trying to calm and control her dog—Gucci settled into wearing the pack and the group took off up the trail. But that was only the first misadventure of the day.

As the hikers were crossing a footbridge, a group of horses and riders came downriver. Gucci loved horses and went wild on the bridge trying to get to them. When she decided that the only way to visit her four-legged friends was through the river, she jumped off the bridge into the water. Gucci escorted the horses and riders down the trail and returned to Hilary shortly. Gucci was soaked, the pack was soaked, and a weekend's worth of dog food was soaked.

That night (Gucci ate people food for dinner), as the campers were preparing to bed down, Hilary faced yet another challenge. Upon entering the tent, Gucci, who had never seen a tent and had no way of knowing that it was simply another type of home, managed to pee quite by accident all over one of the sleeping bags. Perhaps the day had held just one too many new adventures for the dog. She was quickly banished outside for the night.

Gucci curled up outside the tent door and was calm for a while until she heard a mysterious noise—and growled. She continued to growl at every noise, every shadow, and every movement until the sun rose the next morning. None of the campers got much sleep that night.

After this first experience, Hilary decided to car camp with Gucci instead of backpack. She realized that while Gucci had learned to carry a pack, could tolerate a tent with a little practice,

When planning a trip, think about what will be fun for you and your dog.

and could easily be kept on a leash, training her to ignore the night sounds was more than Hilary was willing to do. So she has adapted her trips. Gucci now sleeps inside the protection of their van, where she doesn't have to guard the campers from every sound, bump, and shadow of the night. And nobody has to worry about Gucci's food getting soaked in a river.

Don't let this story scare you away from backpacking or any other kind of camping. Instead, *let it illustrate how important planning can be.*

A dog that isn't used to a pack can get used to one. A dog that loves horses can be trained to stay with the group (or you can put him on a leash) A tent-shy dog can get used to and learn to love sleeping in a tent. Even dogs that jump at every night noise can settle into a sound sleep—all with a little preparation.

The first step is deciding which type of camping will fit you and your dog's personality and temperament. As you read the following information, think about your dog. Is he comfortable around other animals? Does he have a hard time with noise? Does he like riding in the car? Can he easily adapt to new activities? Is he a puppy or an older dog? Do you have the time, energy, and willingness to train him to be comfortable in a situation that may go against his natural temperament? Although most dogs can be trained to enjoy most activities, if you choose a type of camping that will be hard for your dog, you will need to spend more time preparing him for the trip. On the other hand, spending the time to prepare your dog (and yourself) for different adventures will mean that you'll be able to take him just about everywhere.

Car Camping

The most common type of outdoor experience today is car camping. When the weekend arrives, you can throw a tent, sleeping bag, and a few dozen other essential items into the back of the car. You grab your dog's leash and the two of you hit the road. After driving a few hours, you pull into the check-in station at a campground near a great big beautiful river, lake, or desert canyon. You unload all of the gear, set up camp, and settle in for a relaxing weekend. Sounds great.

Advantages
- When you car camp, you experience the outdoors—fresh air, birds singing, nature on your doorstep—without being as completely vulnerable to the elements as you may be with other outdoor adventures. Your car is always right there if the weather gets bad or you have a medical emergency.
- Car camping is inexpensive. Campground fees can run from free to twenty-five dollars a night. Generally, the range is five to fifteen dollars, with some places asking an additional fee for your dog.
- When you car camp in established campgrounds, you have access to running water.
- Bathrooms are available. Some camp areas have only simple outhouses, but many have full bathrooms, including sinks for brushing teeth. Some even have hot showers.

One of the advantages of car camping is being able to bring along lots of gear. Lily loves to fish but hates to clean.
PHOTO COURTESY MARY KROSKE AND JEAN FAIRBANKS

- Family campgrounds often have stores where you can purchase those forgotten items. This can come in handy if you forget matches, your flashlight batteries go dead, or you discover that you can't open that can of dog food bare-handed.
- Many campgrounds are in or on the edge of parks or recreational areas. You'll often find hiking, fishing, boating, or swimming right next door.
- You can take as much gear as you can cram into your vehicle. This means an inflatable mattress for a good night's sleep, a tent tall enough to stand up in, your dog's favorite blanket, a Frisbee, a tennis ball, a tug toy, *and* a bone. You'll also have plenty of room for an ice chest, cold drinks, and lots of fun foods.

- If you're traveling with children as well as your dog, you'll have plenty of room for all of their things, too.
- If you're traveling alone with just yourself and your dog, you may feel less vulnerable in a campground with other people around than you would in the wilderness.
- If you get tired of camp cooking, you can always hop in the car and take a quick jaunt into a neighboring town for pizza.
- If you or your dog have any type of physical limitations, car camping can give you many of the wonderful outdoor experiences without the tremendous physical exertion of a wilderness camping trip.
- Some more elaborate campgrounds also have swimming pools, tennis courts, horseback riding, laundry areas, and more.

Drawbacks

But before you make up your mind that car camping is for you, take a look at the drawbacks.

- Many car-camping areas and campgrounds are like little towns—complete with neighbors, traffic, and noise.
- If your dog is extremely shy or tends to bark a lot at people and activity, this type of camping might create extra stress for both of you.
- While car camping can provide a great outdoor adventure, you won't be getting the full wilderness experience—being out against the elements, person and dog alone in the wild, with the satisfaction of living and surviving with only the food, clothes, and shelter that you can carry on your back.

Backpacking

Unlike car camping, backpacking opens up the experience of the wilderness. When you backpack, you take only what you can carry comfortably. You load up your backpack with the bare minimum—tent, sleeping bag, food, water, basic cooking gear, emergency supplies, and clothing. Your dog's pack is loaded with his food and water. You set off down a trail at daybreak and walk until you reach your destination. Your evening is spent on the basics of survival—setting up camp, cooking, cleaning up, and resting for the next day's leg of the trip. Maybe you pick a spot and just hang out for a few days, enjoying the solitude and quiet. You and your dog get used to a world without cars, people, other dogs, and noise.

Advantages
- It's free (if you backpack in an area that requires a wilderness permit, you may have to pay a few dollars for the permit).
- You are far from everyday headaches—cars, traffic, phones, and other people.
- You leave behind chores, worries, and civilized conventions. You won't have to shower or even comb your hair if you don't want to. For the few days or weeks that you're on the trail, life will take on a new simplicity.
- You'll be moving slowly, at foot speed, through different areas. You and your dog will see nature at a slow, easy pace.
- You and your dog will be getting terrific exercise. You'll be pushing your physical limitations and feeling your sense of self-esteem and self-reliance grow with the experience.
- You and your dog will get closer to nature. You'll be sharing your temporary home with the animals that live year-round in the wilderness—everything from squirrels to bears. And you'll be experiencing nature on her terms.

Drawbacks
Of course, taking nature on nature's terms can have its problems, too.

- Once you are ten miles (or fifteen or twenty miles) away from "civilization," you are really on your own. If it starts raining, you get wet. If you run out of water or forget your matches, you go without. If your dog gets sore paws, he still has to walk on them.
- Backpacking takes careful planning and organization. Throwing a few items together and heading for the trail without careful planning could get you into serious trouble.

Backpacking means carrying all of your gear.
Your dog can help carry her share, too.
PHOTO COURTESY MARY KROSKE AND JEAN FAIRBANKS

- If you are not in good physical shape, backpacking can be not only miserable but dangerous. You need to know and respect your dog's limitations and your own. Even if you're both in great shape, you may still have to deal with achy muscles and sore feet and paws.
- Some dogs cannot carry packs because of physical limitations or size—this means more weight for you to carry.
- If you're going for a few days, you may be able to take along good fresh foods. But for an extended trip, you'll probably have to resort to the freeze-dried variety. The number-one complaint about backpacking is the food.

Walk-in Camping

Walk-in campgrounds are great for the camper who wants to get away from cars and crowds without backpacking into the wilderness. You walk to the camp area down a trail from the parking lot. It's close enough (anywhere from a quarter of a mile to one mile) to your car that you can take a lot more gear than when you backpack, and you have the safety of having a car nearby. Yet you'll feel more like you're "getting away from it all" than if you were car camping. For many campers, the walk-in campground offers the perfect compromise.

Advantages

- The cost is usually less than for car camping, ranging from free to ten dollars per night (walk-in campgrounds often have a small fee for dogs).
- You can take almost as much gear as you can car camping, especially if you're willing to make more than one trip from the car. If you like to take a lot of gear, you can also cart your things down the trail in a wagon, wheelbarrow, or luggage carrier (yes—people really do this).
- Late-night arrivals are less likely when people have to hike into a camp area, creating a quieter and more relaxed overall experience.
- While you're seldom the only camper at a walk-in site, you'll often be one of only a few (although some of the larger walk-in sites do get crowded, especially on busy weekends).
- Many walk-in campgrounds have drinking water and outhouses, so you won't have to carry in water or pack out or bury your waste.
- This type of camping can be especially great if you are traveling with young children (as well as your dog) and want to give them more of a wilderness experience.

Drawbacks

- Walk-in campgrounds are a compromise; they give neither the total convenience of car camping nor the total wilderness experience of backpacking.
- As with car camping, you will probably still have neighbors and activity.
- As with backpacking, if it starts raining, you get wet.

Canoeing, Kayaking, and Rafting

Taking a canoe, kayak, or raft trip with your dog is another way to experience the great outdoors. You can load up your boat with your gear, outfit yourself and your dog with life vests, and head down the river. While you paddle, your dog can take in the scenery and soak up the sunshine. When you pull onto shore to set up camp, your dog can stretch his legs and then help you gather wood for a campfire. You can fix a great meal, set up your tent, and take a hike before the sun sets. If you enjoy fishing, you can cast in a line in the early-morning light before you again head downriver.

Advantages
- Canoeing is usually free—if you have your own canoe and equipment (in some areas, you may have to pay for a wilderness permit or a launching fee).
- Canoes can hold a lot of gear, so you won't have to worry as much about packing lightly.
- Most dogs enjoy traveling by canoe once they are accustomed to it.
- Traveling and camping on a river can offer some majestic scenery.
- As with backpacking, you and your dog will be experiencing nature on her terms.
- Canoeing, while physically strenuous for the paddler, offers you and your dog a good way of getting into the wilderness if your dog cannot backpack. It may also be a good option for the person who cannot comfortably walk long distances carrying a pack.

Drawbacks
- If you or your dog are not comfortable around water, canoeing may not be for you (see Chapters 5, 7, and 9 for tips on getting your dog used to the water, teaching him to swim, and keeping him safe on wet outings).

Canoe or kayak trips are another way of experiencing
the great outdoors with your dog.
PHOTO COURTESY MARY KROSKE AND JEAN FAIRBANKS

- The *initial* outlay for equipment is high. Buying a canoe and other assorted equipment, or even renting, can set you back some bucks.
- Your dog will have to sit still in the canoe for long stretches of time—he may get bored (see Chapter 5 for tips on teaching your dog to ride in a canoe or kayak).
- Canoeing means spending your days on the water, and in warm weather, that usually means lots of mosquitoes.
- You will have to take extra precautions to avoid overexposure to the sun, wind, and other elements.
- If you are not familiar with traveling on water, you will need to learn a lot about currents, weather, and safety before you embark on your trip.

Recreational Vehicles

If you like comfort and convenience, think about traveling in an RV. Whether the vehicle is a smaller-type camper van, a pickup truck, a trailer or full-size motor home, an RV gives you a range of travel and camping options. You can set out for an established campground, or if you have a self-contained vehicle, you can pull off the road where it is legal and have most of the comforts of home. You'll be able to cook on a stove, sleep on a bed, and pull food from a refrigerator. You and your dog will be fully protected from the elements yet have a great base from which to explore.

Advantages

One RV camper said that what she liked best was the overall convenience of this type of travel with a dog. Consider:

- Most RV camping areas allow dogs.
- If the RV has a generator with air-conditioning and heating, you can safely leave your dog for short periods of time while you visit areas where dogs are not allowed.
- If your camping trip is coupled with travel, you'll have the convenience of not having to set up and break down camp each day.
- Many RVs are self-contained, which means that you have your own toilet and can shower without waiting in line.
- You can have a comfortable bed complete with sheets and pillow.
- You are protected from rain, wind, snow, sun, and heat. In fact, you and your dog will be comfortable in most conditions. It's like having your own house on wheels.

Drawbacks

- You will have to drive around in a rather awkward vehicle; it is hard to park at the store when you pick up supplies.
- You will definitely miss out on living with the elements.
- It can be expensive. If you own an RV, you will still have to pay premium campground prices for hookups. If you rent, a full-sized motor home can cost from $80 to $200 a night.

*For some dogs and people, traveling in an RV
means the best of home and camping.*

Bicycle Touring

Bicycle touring is a great way to travel. You spend your days on the road. You move quickly from town to town, seeing, breathing, and feeling the sights. You move faster than on foot, you see things that you'd miss from a car, yet you are still self-sufficient. At night, you can set up camp in a campground or, where it's legal, simply pull off to the side of the road. Of course, your dog can't pedal a bike, and there is no way to make it safe for a dog to run alongside a bike for more than a few miles (that would be an awfully short tour). So how do you take your canine friend along?

Bicycle touring with a dog means that you have to pedal his weight as well as your own. For obvious reasons, this makes it a better option for those of you with smaller dogs. Dogs can be taken along in specially built carriers that attach to the rear rack of the bike. The rack carrier is small and lightweight, but you'll have to build it yourself because a carrier suitable for touring has yet to hit the stores (see Chapter 5 for more information on traveling by bike).

You can also take your dog along in a trailer that is pulled behind your bike. One company, CycleTote, makes trailers specifically for dogs (see Appendix H). Or you can easily adapt a trailer made for pulling children. The trailer provides protection from sun and rain but is a bit awkward to pull down the road.

Advantages
- Bicycling is a great way to travel from place to place. You have freedom of movement, yet you're not confined to a car.
- It's terrific exercise.
- It's a great option if you are traveling with a small dog, an older dog, or a disabled dog. The dog rides while you pedal.
- If you like civilization, you won't have to leave it behind. You'll be able to eat in restaurants, visit tourist areas, and generally see the sights.
- When combined with camping, bicycle touring is an inexpensive way to travel—if you have your own equipment.

Drawbacks
What are the limitations of bicycle touring?

- It's simply not practical with a bigger dog (can you picture yourself hauling a ninety-pound Rottweiler down the road in a bike cart?).
- Your dog will have to be trained to sit quietly for a few hours at a time.
- Your traveling must include a reward for your dog's good behavior—like running and playing at the end of the day.
- If you don't already have the equipment, getting set up for bicycle touring can be costly.
- Bicycling with a dog in a carrier is only suitable for road travel. Trying to go on dirt roads or off-road would be dangerous for you and uncomfortable for your dog.

Your small dog can share your bike-touring adventure in a custom-built carrier.

Tent Cabins

Many private and some state camp areas rent tent cabins. National parks usually have tent cabins, too, but many do not allow dogs. If you don't have much camping gear, this may be a good option. Basic shelter is provided, and setting up camp is easy—just unload the car and spread your sleeping bag. You'll have a warm, weather-tight place to spend your nights.

Advantages

- All you need is basic gear—sleeping bag or blankets, cooking equipment, and dog supplies—a good option if you don't have a tent or backpacking gear.
- Many places with tent cabins have fully equipped campgrounds, including hot showers, laundry facilities, and swimming pools.
- Usually tent cabins start at around twenty-five dollars per night. And, while this is not cheap, it may still be less expensive than outfitting yourself with a tent, a tarp, a sleeping pad, and a backpack.

Drawbacks
- Some places allow only smaller dogs; check this out carefully.
- You will have few of the conveniences of RV travel (no air-conditioned home-on-wheels in which to leave your dog while you visit the "no-dogs-allowed" areas), but many of the restrictions, such as staying in primarily populated areas.

Dog Camps

Dog camps are a relatively new phenomenon that combine all of the fun of the more traditional summer camp with a resort-like atmosphere. Every activity is geared toward you and your dog. If you choose a dog camp, your weekend or week-long experience may unfold something like this: You'll arrive at camp and check into your own single or double cabin. Your day will be filled with activities such as agility workshops (where your dog can learn to run an obstacle course complete with jumps, tunnels, and teeter-totters), obedience training, health-care classes, Frisbee competitions, and herding workshops. If organized activities aren't for you, you'll still be spending time in a place where dogs are not only allowed, but welcomed, pampered, and cherished. You can take walks, go for a swim, or just spend time together. And, at the end of the day, your meal will be cooked for you!

Advantages
For some people, this may seem like a dream vacation:
- You and your dog get to spend your whole time together. You can eat, sleep, and play without some of the restrictions that you may find in other camping areas.
- You'll be around other dogs and their people. This is especially great if your dog likes to play with other dogs. It can also be fun for you to meet other people who like to be around dogs as much as you do.
- The entire time is set up for both your own and your dog's enjoyment. You'll have a chance to choose activities that are tailor-made for dogs and people.
- You'll sleep in a comfortable cabin.

Dog camps offer a variety of activities, from agility classes to hiking and swimming.
PHOTO BY LARRY MICHAEL; COURTESY DOG DAYS OF WISCONSIN

- It's easy—all of your planning and preparation are done for you. You and your dog simply show up.
- If you're looking for a Club Med-type experience for you and your dog, this type of camping is for you.

Drawbacks
- It's really more of a resort vacation experience than a camping trip.
- It is completely dog-focused and may not be the best option if you are looking for a family vacation.
- Prices vary but generally run $400 to $500 for a week. This may seem a little steep until you break it down into food, lodging, and activities per day.
- If your dog doesn't get along with other dogs, it may not be such a fun experience for either of you.
- If you like your dog but not necessarily other people's dogs, this may not be for you either.
- If you haven't crossed the line from dog owner to dog fanatic, you may burn out before the trip is over.

(For a list of dog camps, see Appendix E. You may also find dog camps advertised in dog magazines.)

How to Decide What's Right for You and Your Dog

While these descriptions can give you an idea of each type of camping, they are by no means exhaustive. There are as many variations in camping as there are people and dogs. For example, you can take a backpacking trip in the snow or through the desert, you can canoe down a river or across a lake, and you can drive your full-sized RV to a KOA campground or your four-wheel-drive truck to a remote wilderness area. All have their advantages and disadvantages, and as you are deciding which adventure is right for you and your dog, you have to consider many factors. Most important, think about your dog in the process. While he may not be able to say, "Hey, I'd really like to try out canoeing," you can include his personality, age, physical needs, and temperament in the decision-making criteria. Your dog can greatly enhance or detract from the enjoyment of your trip.

THE CAMPING QUIZ

Still not sure which type of camping is right for you both? Try this quick check test to help you decide.

Answer the following questions about *you and your family*:

Yes   No

___   ___   1. Are you new to camping?

___   ___   2. Do you want the convenience of running water and bathrooms?

___   ___   3. Do you like the idea of having everything you could possibly need?

___   ___   4. Do you have physical limitations that make it hard for you to enjoy strenuous activity?

___   ___   5. Do you feel okay about sharing your nature experience with other people?

___   ___   6. Do you want to leave cars and other conveniences of everyday life behind?

___   ___   7. Are you in good physical shape?

___   ___   8. Do you like the idea of traveling miles with twenty-five pounds or more on your back?

___   ___   9. Do you own or have access to specialized equipment?

___   ___   10. Do you crave solitude and challenge?

Answer these questions about *your dog*:

Yes   No

___   ___   1. Does your dog like people?

___   ___   2. Does your dog get along with other dogs?

___   ___   3. Is your dog fairly well mannered around people and dogs?

___   ___   4. Does your dog have any physical limitations (including being younger or older) that would make it hard for him to enjoy strenuous activity?

___   ___   5. Is your dog in good physical shape?

___   ___   6. Is your dog able to carry a dog pack?

___   ___   7. Does your dog adapt well to new and different surroundings?

___   ___   8. Does your dog enjoy adventure?

(TEST SCORING ON NEXT PAGE)

THE CAMPING QUIZ:
TEST SCORING

FOR YOU:

Yes to questions 1-5—you'll probably enjoy car camping, RV camping, or tent cabins.

Yes to questions 6-10—you'll probably enjoy backpacking or walk-in campgrounds.

FOR YOUR DOG:

Yes to questions 1-4—Your dog will probably enjoy car camping, RV camping, or tent cabins.

Yes to questions 5-8—Your dog will probably enjoy backpacking or walk-in campgrounds.

(If you answer yes to number 4 for either you or your dog but still want a wilderness experience, consider a canoe trip. If you answer yes to number 4 for just your dog, consider bicycle touring.)

CHAPTER TWO

DECIDING WHERE TO GO

One of my first camping trips with dogs was with my dog
Charlie. Of course, I knew that many places did not allow
dogs. Even in our daily walks around town, we'd encountered
numerous "NO DOGS ALLOWED" signs. I knew to plan ahead,
and so I called the headquarters at Andrew Molera State Park
on the Big Sur coast in California.

"Yup," the ranger said, "no problem bringing your dog. They
do have to be on leash and we charge one dollar per day for dogs."

That sounded great. I'd visited the park a few years earlier
and knew about the long, white, sandy beach. The river running
through the campground would be perfect for evening walks.
And the park had an extensive series of hiking trails leading
from the coast, through the grasslands and oak trees, to red-
wood forests—a great place to cruise with a dog.

When we got to the campground, I set up camp and we
headed to the beach for a quick romp before dinner. Just as we
reached the trail leading to the white dunes, I saw a sign for
beach restrictions—"NO DOGS ALLOWED ON THE BEACH."

Call ahead to make sure this doesn't happen to you!

Giving a sigh, Charlie and I turned around and headed toward the river. We could take a walk along the banks, then head back to camp for dinner. As we approached the trail weaving by the riverbank, another sign loomed ahead—"NO DOGS ALLOWED."

Not one to give up easily, I shrugged my shoulders and headed back to the trail behind the campground. We could take a short walk up the trail and get a feel for the next day's longer hike. As we approached that trailhead, well, you guessed it—"NO DOGS ALLOWED."

The ranger had said that dogs were allowed in the campground—no problem. What he had neglected to mention (and I, being new to camping with my dog, didn't know to ask) was that the campground was the *only* place in the immediate area where dogs *were* allowed.

Fortunately, this story had a happy ending. The next morning, we moved our camp to a nearby national forest where Charlie and I could romp and hike with complete freedom. The obvious moral of this story: Finding out if dogs are allowed in the campground is only the first step.

There are really two parts to figuring out where to go camping with your dog—finding the places that offer you the kind of overall experience you're looking for, and figuring out where dogs are allowed. Choosing a place to camp involves exploring both of these options, then finding where the two meet.

Start with the Overall Experience

Think about where you want to travel. How much time do you have? Where will you and your dog most enjoy spending time—the desert, the beach, or the mountains? Do you want to hike? And if so, do you want to be near water or snow? The key is to know yourself, to know your dog, and to choose an adventure that will suit you both. Consider the following:

Creature Comforts. Are you looking for the great wilderness experience? Or are you more interested in the outdoor adventure with the creature comforts of home—running water, flush toilets, showers? Consider what your dog would enjoy most too.

Are there certain creature comforts that you would rather not live without while camping?

Types of Activity. Perhaps you'd like to hike or fish. Maybe you want to camp near a beach and take long walks by the ocean with your canine friend. Or would you rather see local sights, visit tourist areas, and eat in outdoor cafes along the way?

Scenic Requirements. Our friend Anne finds great comfort on the high desert with the silent nights and quiet aliveness. I'm never more at home and relaxed than when I'm near a rushing river or crashing waves. Moving water makes a trip come alive for me. Melanee likes open meadows and oak trees. Bruce is enamored with giant redwoods. What appeals to you? Do you want to explore new areas? Or would you rather relax with what you know?

Types of Terrain. If you are simply camping and enjoying the sights from the comfort of your campsite, terrain may only be a factor in the scenic requirements. But if you're planning to hike or explore, it is important to consider the lay of the land. Is your dog used to steep hikes and altitude? Can he swim? What about those shale rocks on soft paws? I know several people who enjoy rock climbing and who include their dogs in their quest to reach the highest peak. Gary once took his dog, Rainier, up a chimney climb. Rainier sat nervously in Gary's lap as Gary slowly inched his way to the top. When they reached their destination, both dog and man were exhilarated from the experience. For some, this kind of adventure is more frightening than fun; for others, it's the experience of a lifetime. What are you looking for? A challenging but manageable hike? Perhaps an adventurous mountain bike ride? A comfortable walk to a swimming hole? Will your adventure leave you feeling exhilarated or too sore to move for days after? Think about the terrain. Is it hilly or mountainous? Are there clifflike peaks? Are there open meadows or sleepy, wooded trails? Are there desert sand dunes or melting snowdrifts?

Accessibility. Along with terrain, consider whether the campground is easily accessible. How will you and your camping companions reach the campsite? Find out about road and trail conditions. I've been to state campgrounds that can only be reached by four-wheel-drive. Other questions of accessibility include your human and dog limitations. Are you in a wheelchair? Does your dog have arthritis? Backpacking might not be a great idea if you have a bad back. A canoe trip wouldn't be the best choice if your dog gets seasick.

Weather. What time of year are you planning your trip? What type of weather should you expect? Think about how temperature, humidity, and windchill will influence your plans, comfort, and needs. The Arizona desert in mid-July is not a good choice if you are traveling with an Alaskan Malamute. Conversely, a cross-country ski trip in early January could be pretty rough on a Whippet. Equally as important is the type of equipment you have. Summer sleeping bags are not sufficient in early spring or late fall in the High Sierras. And a family-style tent (minus the rain fly) can make camping in the rainy season a bit soggy.

Dog Temperament. Along with your dog's physical needs, consider his temperament. My dog Charlie was content in the wilderness and in quiet areas. He was also a tireless hiker. But he came to me afraid of people and activity, and even after years of socialization and training, he was never completely comfortable around other people and dogs. My current dog Blue is just the opposite. She loves people and other dogs, and because she's a Border Collie, she needs constant work. She also has hip dysplasia and cannot tolerate super strenuous activity. Charlie was ideally suited for long, lonely backpacking trips but would have been one miserable pup at a dog camp. Blue could never handle the physical challenge of a backpacking trip, yet she would thrive on the type of constant "work" and activity offered at dog camps.

People Temperament. Equally important is your temperament and that of the other human campers on your trip. While some people are happy sleeping on the ground and burying their excrement, others cannot live without running water and their favorite feather pillow.

Consider your dog's personality when choosing a camping trip.
For some dogs, like Tougher, a climbing adventure is a real tail wagger.
PHOTO COURTESY EUGENE BUSH AND CATHERINE TOLDI

Where Your Dog Is Welcome

National Forests

National forests can be a gold mine for the dog lover. Not only are dogs generally allowed, they are often permitted off leash. (Read Chapter 6 before you let your dog off leash in a national forest, or anywhere else.) National forests are usually less crowded than national parks and state parks. They typically have both developed and undeveloped camp areas and have low-cost camping fees.

National Parks

Unlike national forests, national parks are not always a great place to take dogs. Some do allow dogs in the camping areas, but dogs are rarely allowed on trails, even on leash. (You will find a few notable exceptions to this in the more remote national parks in Alaska.) National parks also are more crowded and pricey than national forests. They do, however, have some of the most wondrous sights—giant redwoods, grand canyons, and cascading waterfalls, to name just a few.

If you choose to visit a national park with your dog, you may want to check out dog-friendly camp areas outside the park boundaries. You may also be able to find a dog day-care or a kennel to board your dog while you explore the dog-prohibited areas within the park.

Bureau of Land Management (BLM) Lands

BLM lands are public lands that include camping and hiking areas. BLM campgrounds usually are remote and offer limited facilities. Dogs are generally allowed on leash in developed areas and off leash in undeveloped areas. BLM lands include some of the most scenic areas in the United States.

National forests are a gold mine for the canine camper.
PHOTO COURTESY PENNY AND MIKE BROZDA

State and Local Parks

Some state and county parks and camp areas allow dogs and others do not. Rules about dogs vary from park to park and state to state. Your best bet is to call the park and ask if dogs are allowed. Remember to ask if dogs are allowed on trails and in surrounding areas, too.

Private Campgrounds

Private campgrounds vary in their rules about dogs. Many, but not all, allow small dogs. The definition of a small dog differs from place to place, but usually a dog less than thirty pounds is considered small. Some allow bigger dogs "as long as they are well behaved." Many private campgrounds cater to RV travelers and not only allow dogs, but have fun and convenient facilities for people, too—like swimming pools and stores. Some are located in recreational areas or near national forests and national parks.

 Paw Note: *For addresses and phone numbers of national forest, BLM, national park, and state park regional contacts and a list of camping guidebooks, see Appendices A, B, C, D, and F.*

Finding the Perfect Spot

You have a vision in your head. Perhaps it's a weekend backpacking trip to a river or lake. Maybe you're thinking about a stay in a state park with plenty of big trees and nature walks. You have an idea of where your dog will be welcome. Now it's time to get specific and find your perfect spot.

Talk with Other Campers

One of the best ways to find the right campground is to talk with other people who camp with dogs. Ask your friends. Ask your friend's friends. Ask the people who work at your local outdoor-equipment store. Check with the people at your local animal-

supply store. Ask your veterinarian and your dog trainer. You'll
be surprised how many people know the perfect spots to camp
with dogs.

Search through Guidebooks

There are more camping guidebooks with extensive listings
of campgrounds than needles on pine trees. Some are very good,
and many of them tell you if dogs are allowed. Some are exclusively private (like KOA listings) or exclusively public (like
national forest listings). Others try to be comprehensive within
a region, and some list camping sites as well as other places that
are geared specifically for dogs and their people. See Appendix F
for some especially helpful guidebooks, keeping in mind that
there are many more. Visit your local library or bookstore to find
guidebooks specific to the area that you would like to visit. Your
local reference librarian is often a wealth of information and can
show you guides to forests, parks, wilderness areas, and more.

Check Online Resources

Going online with your computer is another way to find
places to camp. The Internet is a vast source of information for
both campers and dog lovers—although you have to be creative
to find where the two meet.

For information about a specific place, you can often go
directly to a web site. For example, if you are looking for a
campground within the Montana BLM lands, you can go to the
national web site—www.blm.gov—to find the state-specific site
and information. The same is true for national forests and
many state parks. Some online addresses are listed in the
appendices, but you can also do a subject or name search to find
national and state camping areas.

You might also look in the dog or outdoor-travel-specific
chat rooms, news groups, and bulletin boards and ask other dog
people where they go camping with their dogs. Or you can look
up dog and travel magazines, see if they have a homepage, and
browse through their information. You can check out clubs and

organizations. You can also hook into commercial sources like Great Outdoor Recreation Pages (GORP) at www.gorp.com, where you can get information about lots of different types of outdoor adventures.

Contact Local Organizations

Another source of information is clubs and organizations. For example, the Sierra Club chapter in Los Angeles has a group called the K-9 Hikers Committee, a club for people who like to experience the outdoors with their dogs. This is a hiking group, but where you find people hiking with their dogs, you're bound to find them camping as well.

Doublecheck, Ask Questions, and Make Sure

If you find a place in a guidebook that seems great or a friend tells you of a perfect campground, you still need to investigate before you go. Rules and regulations about dogs are ever-changing. A place that accepted dogs last year might not this year. Call ahead and check it out.

Questions to Ask When You Contact a Campground

1. Are dogs allowed in the campground? Are they allowed in only some areas? On trails? On beaches? On leash? Off leash?
2. Are there any size restrictions? (Some places only allow smaller dogs.)
3. Are there other rules or restrictions regarding dogs? (Such as those about quiet times, leashes, and where the dog sleeps.)
4. Do you charge additional fees for dogs? What are they?
5. Do I need proof of vaccinations or a health certificate?
6. Do there tend to be a lot of dogs in the camp area?
7. What kind of wildlife is in the area? Are there any plants or animals to be aware of when camping with a dog? (Like poison oak or rattlesnakes.)
8. Is there running water? Other facilities?
9. Are reservations needed? A deposit? Permits?

CHAPTER THREE

GETTING INTO SHAPE

BJ was a tough dog. She went trail running three times a week, played Frisbee and ball on the other days, and had been on many backpacking trips. But even a dog that is in great shape may run into problems if he is not conditioned for the specific demands of the upcoming adventure.

BJ and her people were in the Granite Lake area of the Trinity Alps, above treeline at about 9,000 feet. The first few days had been more strenuous than BJ was accustomed to—a steep hike in, high altitude, and plenty of active day hikes. In addition, it was very cold at night. BJ was showing signs of fatigue. BJ's people weren't sure if it was the altitude, the amount of activity, or the cold nights that were affecting her the most. They tried keeping her warmer at night and feeding her extra food.

The most serious problem came the morning they planned to leave. BJ's people packed up their gear, preparing to head the five miles back down to their car. At first they noticed that BJ wasn't getting up or moving. Was she just tired? They tried calling her and bribing her with treats, but BJ wouldn't budge. On closer inspection, they discovered the problem. BJ not only was exhausted, but her pads had been cut by the shale that they had been hiking over the day before. BJ was a sensible dog—she was not going to walk out while her feet were hurting!

The only way to get BJ down the mountain was to carry her. But how do you safely carry a sixty-five-pound lab mix down a steep trail? By putting her into a pack, of course. BJ rode in style, hoisted upon her person's back, the entire five miles to the car.

If you start a trip by asking your dog to do more than she is able, you may end up carrying her on the way out.
PHOTO COURTESY VAL LEOFFLER

BJ's story is not uncommon. Dogs get tired, sore, fatigued, and injured—just like people. But unlike people, dogs don't usually pace themselves for the long haul. A dog frequently exhausts his energy and strength in the excitement of the first few miles of a hike. Depending on the size of the dog, he may have to take two or three steps for each one of yours. Even a dog like BJ, who was in good shape for everyday life, can become fatigued under the strenuous conditions of backpacking or hiking, especially over rough or hilly terrain or at higher altitudes. A dog off leash will often run up and down the trails, covering more than twice as much territory as their human counterparts.

BJ was the exceptional type of dog, who stopped when she reached her limit and refused to go on. Many dogs, however, will keep going as long as their people are moving, wanting to keep up or just wanting to please. Unfortunately, a dog that pushes beyond his limits faces countless risks—from sore muscles to serious injury. In extreme cases, a dog may overdo to the point of permanent injury or even death.

Getting your dog in shape, knowing his limits, and planning a trip accordingly are important components of getting ready to head out on your camping excursion. You'll need to know how to get your dog into shape, and you'll need to know the general signs of fatigue to make sure that your dog is not overdoing it.

Ten Steps for Getting Your Dog into Shape

1. Decide Just How Physically Fit Your Dog Needs to Be

What kind of trip are you planning? Are you going backpacking or on a weekend car-camping trip? For car camping, you may want to prepare for day hikes with or without your dog carrying a pack. For a weekend trip that includes mountain biking, you will need to make sure that both you and your dog are in top physical shape. If your dog will be off leash, he may cover two to three times the distance that you do. Plan accordingly.

Some dogs will need more conditioning than others.

2.   Assess Your Dog's Condition

Ask yourself honestly: Is my dog a couch potato? Does he get regular exercise? How much? How will it compare to the exercise that he'll get on our camping trip? Also consider the type of dog you have. In general, dogs with long, straight legs can cover more territory comfortably than dogs with shorter legs. Larger dogs are better suited to carrying their own pack. (It's best not to have a dog under 30 pounds carry a pack.)

3.   Check with Your Veterinarian

It is always a good idea to check with your veterinarian before you start your dog on a conditioning program. You'll want to have the veterinarian assess your dog's heart, his respiratory system, his muscular and skeletal condition, and his general health. Ask your veterinarian for suggestions about a conditioning program. Also, ask if your dog's diet is appropriate for the amount of exercise he will be getting. Dogs that are getting an increased amount of exercise may need to eat a higher-energy or higher-fat diet. If your dog has special needs, your veterinarian will be able to help you get your dog in shape safely.

4. Start Early

It's never too early to get into shape. As with people, you'll need to allow a few weeks to a few months depending on the shape your dog is in now. Even if you are planning a trip with only moderate activity, start working out at least six weeks before your trip if your dog is out of shape.

5. Build Up Slowly

Start your dog off gradually, only doing as much as he is able to do comfortably. After a week or two of light activity, you can safely add a few minutes a day to your dog's exercise program. For example, if your dog does not get much exercise now, start with a ten- or fifteen-minute walk a day for the first week or so. Then add five minutes every few days until you are up to four to six miles at a brisk pace. Then add in hills, rougher terrain, and longer distances. As with people, alternating long, steady distances with short bursts of strenuous activity will develop the muscular, skeletal, and cardiovascular systems evenly.

Start your dog's conditioning program early.

6. Watch for Signs of Fatigue

I had a dog named Moose when I was a teenager. Moose was an incredibly independent dog. When we would go on hikes, Moose would walk down the path for about forty-five minutes. Then he would find a nice shady spot, where he would proceed to lie down and rest for ten or fifteen minutes. When he was through resting, he would get up, shake off, and give a little bark to let me know that he was ready to continue.

Moose decided when he needed to rest and he communicated it clearly. But many dogs don't communicate that clearly when they need to rest. In fact, most dogs will go past their limits to please their people. You need to be aware of your dog's fatigue level and stop before he gets too tired. If your dog shows signs of fatigue, he has already been pushed beyond his physical limits. Common signs of fatigue are the dog slowing down, stopping often to rest, or losing enthusiasm for the activity. If you notice any of these signs, stop the activity for the day. If your dog starts to limp, pants heavily, or is taking air in short, raspy breaths, stop immediately. Your dog may be close to collapse. If your dog seems slow or tired the next day, give him a break then, too. Dogs get tired and sore just like people.

7. Set Realistic Goals

Pacing is the key. Don't start out too fast or increase the amount of exercise too quickly for your dog. If you adopt the old (and grossly misinformed) attitude of no pain, no gain, you're likely to end up with no companion or, at the least, an unwilling companion. Your dog may be willing to follow you to the ends of the earth on that first day out running, but if you overdo, your dog may only run as far as under the bed when you bring out the leash the next day.

The keys to success: start slowly, pace yourself and your dog, and make it fun.

8. Choose an Activity You'll Both Enjoy

How can you get your dog into shape? Which types of activities are best? Should you try jogging, walking, or swimming?

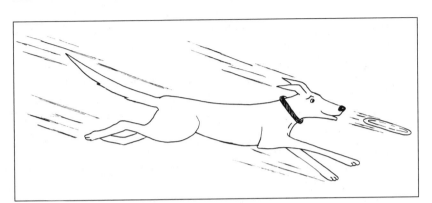

*Flying through the air! Frisbee and ball play are
great ways to get your dog into shape.*

The best activities to use to get your dog into shape are those that you both enjoy. If you and your dog enjoy the time together, you are more likely to stick with it! A dog is almost always ready to play, run, and have a good time. It's the people who often hold him back. Getting into shape takes time and perseverance.

Vary the activities. For people, this is sometimes called cross training. You may want to walk three times a week and play ball twice a week. Or, if your dog is a swimmer, try swimming three days a week and jogging two. Varying the activities helps build muscular strength and stamina faster, with a lower risk of injury.

Here is a partial list of fun activities and exercise that will get both you and your dog into shape:

- **Walking.** This is the all-time favorite pastime for canines and their human companions. It's easy, it's cheap, and it requires only a pair of sturdy shoes, a leash, and a pooper-scooper or plastic bag. You can take neighborhood walks or head for local hiking trails. When you walk for exercise, keep up a good pace, slowly increase the length of the walks, and head for increasingly hilly terrain. Have fun exploring new places.

- **Jogging.** Dogs make great jogging companions and offer a sense of protection for people who jog alone. Jogging is a quick and efficient exercise and a good way for both you and your dog to get into shape with limited time. A word of caution: Don't jog long distances with your dog on sidewalks and streets. Dogs are susceptible to strain on their joints and bones from running on hard surfaces, and they don't have the extra protection and padding offered by a good pair of running shoes. Also, puppies less than a year of age should not jog or run long distances because their bones are still forming and jogging might cause structural damage.

- **Bicycling.** Many dogs think that running next to a bicycle is the greatest fun around. You can carefully train your dog to run on a leash next to your bike. Never attach the leash to the handlebars or to the frame of the bike. If you hold the leash in your hands, do not loop it around your wrist. Hold it so that you can let go quickly to prevent an accident.

  Or try a product such as The Springer or K9 Cruiser. These devices attach to the bicycle frame, leaving both of your hands free for steering and braking. These products keep the dog safely away from the wheels and prevent him from running in front of the bike. The Springer also has a safety release that will help prevent your dog from getting tangled on a post or branch. A word of caution: Only use a flat-buckle collar, a halter, or harness—never a choke chain or prong collar—with these products. When bicycling, you can slow or quicken your pace easily to match that of your dog. As with jogging, use caution when riding with your dog on hard surfaces and don't run puppies that are less than a year old. And, remember, he is running, while you are cruising along on two wheels—don't overdo.

- **Swimming.** Swimming is great exercise for dogs and people alike. It helps build endurance and strength without stressing joints. If you have access to a pool, lake, or pond that is safe for swimming, and if your dog likes water, you're set. Make sure that the water is flat or slow-moving without underwater hidden obstacles, and that it isn't too cold. If your dog shivers when he exits the water, it may be too cold.

> **Paw Note:** *Dogs can easily overdo swimming and a tired dog has a higher risk of drowning. See Chapters 7 and 9 for more instructions about teaching your dog to swim and water safety. Use caution and know your dog's limits.*

- **Retrieving.** Does your dog like to play retrieving games? Tossing a tennis ball or Frisbee for your dog can keep him running with little effort on your part. For a variation that gets your dog moving but saves your arm, use a tennis racket to hit the ball, or try a tennis ball launcher made for retrieving dogs. Tennis ball launchers are often advertised in the back of dog magazines.
- **Obedience Training.** Not only will your dog get a physical workout, but a mental one as well. You may want to work with your dog on your own, or for socialization and structure, you may want to join a local dog-training class. Classes help your dog become accustomed to listening to you around other animals. Sometimes it is easier to be motivated to train your dog in a class. If you can't find a class or you would rather work with your dog on your own, use a good training book as a guide. (See Chapter 6 for more about training and classes. See Appendix G for some good training books.)
- **Agility Training.** Agility is a growing sport among dog enthusiasts and is great exercise for dogs. Dogs learn to dash through tunnels, leap over jumps, and climb structures. In fact, agility exercises are a great way to help your dog get ready for outdoor excursions. The balance-beam exercise can help your dog feel more secure walking across a log over a stream, and the A-frame exercise is great for dogs

Agility training can help condition your dog for camping trips.
PHOTO BY LARRY MICHAEL; COURTESY DOG DAYS OF WISCONSIN

Agility exercises can also help your dog be sure-footed on stream crossings and other camping adventures.
PHOTO COURTESY PENNY AND MIKE BROZDA

that will have to boulder scramble. Plus, it's great fun. Look for a qualified agility instructor in your area, or review the agility books listed in Appendix G. Before starting your dog in agility work, always check with your veterinarian.

These are just a few of the many activities that you and your dog can do together to get into shape. You probably have other activities that you both like to do. Develop your own list and start training and conditioning today.

9.   Toughen Up the Paws

If you are planning to hike, your dog's paws may need to be toughened up slowly to avoid raw and bleeding pads on the trail. Unless your dog is accustomed to long hikes or is a working dog (such as a ranch dog), you will need to take action to ensure that your dog's paws don't get blisters.

Even experienced canine campers like Kendall and Chako will need to have tough paws when walking over rough terrain.
PHOTO COURTESY CALLY HABER

You can help your dog to toughen up his paws naturally by having him walk on rougher surfaces and trails. This will allow him to slowly build up his pads. Another option is to use a commercial pad toughener. This is a cream or lotion that was originally developed for hunting dogs. It works quite well, but you must read and follow the directions carefully. Many pad tougheners are toxic if not used correctly. There are several different brands available at pet-supply stores or through mail-order catalogs.

A homemade version of the commercial pad toughener is to soak your dog's paws in black tea. Use one tea bag with about one-quarter cup of boiling water and let it steep until the tea is very strong. After the tea cools, soak each paw for about three minutes. The tannic acid in the tea makes paws tougher after just one soaking. You can do this on the trail, too.

If you are doing a lot of hiking or walking in rougher environments, such as over shale, hot sand, or snow, take along a set of dog boots to protect your dog's feet, even if his pads have been toughened. You and your dog will be a lot happier if you prevent sore pads. (For more about dog boots, see Chapter 4.)

10. Play It Safe

No matter what activity you choose for play and exercise with your dog, always keep his best interests in mind. Don't ask your dog to do activities that may cause injury and don't ask him to work too hard or to overdo. Always use common sense.

CHAPTER FOUR

PLANNING WHAT TO TAKE

Taking the right supplies is as essential to having a good camping trip as choosing the right spot and getting into shape. What you bring is what you have. Planning is everything! What will happen if you bring too little? Consider:

- A hungry dog, a can of dog food, and no can opener.
- A dog covered in ticks, but no comb, tweezers, or repellent.
- Sore and tender paws and a ten-mile hike back to the car.
- A smelly, muddy pup, no dog bath and a tent that you both share.

Of course, some people opt for "taking everything you can stuff into the car and then some," hoping to have what they need. But by getting specific and organized, you can pack lightly—which has some very distinct advantages. If you take only what you need, you won't have to worry about packing, unpacking, organizing, and keeping track of items that you may never use. Nor will you have to clean and store the extra supplies when you return home. And you'll avoid having almost everything you could ever want—except what you need.

No matter what type of camping trip you are taking, your needs and your dog's will fall into the following basic categories: shelter, sleeping gear, clothing, food, grooming and bathroom supplies, other dog gear, hiking and packing equipment, toys and recreational gear, emergency supplies, and a few miscellaneous items that you won't want to leave home without.

A Word About Cost

Completely outfitting yourself and your dog for camping could cost anywhere from a couple of hundred dollars to a few thousand or more. Of course, you may be able to borrow equipment from friends or family if you're new to camping and are not sure you'll like the experience. Or you could rent a tent and other essentials from your local outdoor store. Once the camping bug bites, however, you'll be better off having your own supplies. In some cases, how much money you spend can make a difference. For example, if you are climbing the highest peaks and need extreme weather protection, you'll want gear that will hold up. But for most vacation and weekend camping trips, you won't need to spend a fortune.

Shelter

No matter what type of camping you are planning to do, you and your dog will need good, solid shelter. Some people like the idea of sleeping outside under the stars—which is great when the conditions are right. But with bugs, bears, and the whims of weather, having good shelter is essential—even if you end up with the stars as your ceiling.

Your choices for shelter are pretty obvious. If you are traveling in an RV or staying in a tent cabin, your home away from home is predetermined. Otherwise you will need a good tent. Tents come in all sizes and shapes. The one you choose will depend on the size you need, the place you'll be camping, and the type of weather you may encounter. Envision the worst possible weather conditions for your trip, then get a tent that will

Make sure that you have enough room in your tent
for you, your dog, and your gear.
PHOTO COURTESY PENNY AND MIKE BROZDA

hold up well under conditions even worse than what you imagine. For example, if you expect moderate weather and the worst would be a little rain, plan for a torrential downpour. One of the fundamental laws of outdoor adventure is: *If you're prepared, you'll never need it. If you're not, you'll need it for sure.*

Paw Note: *We strongly recommend that you have your dog sleep in your tent, RV, or cabin rather than leaving him tied up outside or locked in your car. He will be more comfortable, protected from the elements, safe from predators, and less likely to get riled by night sounds.*

A fundamental law of outdoor adventure:
If you're prepared, you'll never need it. If you're not, you'll need it for sure.

Here are a few other thoughts for selecting a tent when you camp with a dog:

- For backpacking, keep in mind that while you want the lightest and smallest tent practical, you'll be sharing it with your dog. Pick one that is big enough for both of you, and make sure that it is sturdy and secure.
- For car camping, you will have a lot more choices. Some people like a tent big enough in which to stand up and prefer the luxury of a cabin-style tent. These are great if you want extra space or if you're camping with young kids as well as dogs. You can really set it up as a home away from home.
- If you are traveling with your family, another option is to use two smaller tents—one for the adults and a separate one for the older kids. That way you can all have a little

extra room and privacy. Of course, you'll have to argue over who gets to sleep with the dog!

- Look for the amount of weather protection you need for the least cost. Dog claws are hard on tent floors, and you may need to replace the tent a lot sooner than if you were camping without dogs. My first tent—before I started tent camping with dogs—lasted through fifteen years of rough camping. Now, with dogs added to the equation, three to five years is a good life span for a tent.
- You can extend your tent's life by covering the floor with a tarp, which will help protect it from dog dirt and claws. Also, you will want to have a towel and a good dog brush along to clean the camping dirt off your dog before he enters the tent for the night.

Getting Your Dog Used to the Tent

Dogs that have never slept in a tent may be nervous the first time. Use these tips to get your dog used to the tent— before you hit the camping trail:

1. Set your tent up in a place familiar to your dog (your backyard or even your living-room floor). Let your dog sniff and explore the tent.
2. Put your dog's bed or a familiar blanket or towel inside the tent. Crawl in with a handful of treats and call your dog.
3. When your dog comes inside, praise him and give him a treat. Have your dog lie on his bed. Again praise him and give him another treat.
4. Repeat this several times, leaving the door to the tent open so that your dog can go in and out easily.
5. When your dog is comfortable entering the tent and knows his place (on his bed), have him come inside with you. Close the flap, and hang out for a little while, with your dog staying quietly on his bed. Read a book or do a crossword puzzle.
6. Teach your dog from the start that the tent is a place to be quiet and calm, not a place to play or get rowdy. This will save you a few headaches later on.

Your dog's sleeping comfort is as essential as your own.
PHOTO COURTESY MARY KROSKE AND JEAN FAIRBANKS

Some dogs take to a tent right away, while others may be timid or even frightened. If you don't know how your dog will react, take it slowly and offer praise and rewards for each small success. Soon your dog will figure out that this is just another great place to hang out with you.

Sleeping Gear

Comfortable bedding for you and your dog are essential for any camping trip. A sleepless night can put a serious damper on an otherwise wonderful adventure. And remember—your dog's sleeping comfort is as essential as your own.

Dogs that usually sleep indoors may be particularly cold at night. Don't expect your dog to sleep directly on the floor of your tent without any insulation from the cold ground. If you can, take along your dog's regular bed—he'll appreciate the familiarity.

For backpacking, you can take a child's sleeping bag or a small, easy-to-roll dog bed. You can also have your dog share your sleeping pad and bag. If you don't mind a few dog hairs on your clothes, your down jacket or parka can double as a dog bed. Many people will make faces of horror at this suggestion. "Not my expensive parka!" But I spent years backpacking with my dog Charlie, and he always slept on my down jacket. He was comforted by my smell on his makeshift bed and was warm through the night. The jacket never suffered any harm.

Your own sleeping equipment can be as simple as a sleeping bag and an Ensolite pad or as elaborate as a cot complete with sheets and pillow. Once again, this depends on the type of camping you're doing and on your own comfort zone. Here are a few additional thoughts on choosing sleeping gear:

- Look for a bag made of sturdy material. Some bags have a thin nylon shell that one misplaced dog nail will easily rip. Get a bag with a heavy outer shell—it will last longer.
- Remember your dog when you choose padding. An inexpensive, inflatable mattress may be comfortable, but it also may start leaking the first time your dog treads on it. Instead, use an Ensolite pad (these give good protection from the cold, but not much padding) or a Therm-a-Rest pad (this gives the comfort of air cushioning, the warmth of Ensolite, and the durability of the canvas shell).
- An alternative for car camping is a foam egg-crate pad. You can buy a more expensive version from upscale camping stores and catalogs (such as L. L. Bean). Or check out your local variety store (such as K-Mart) for egg-crate mattress pads. These are inexpensive and work well. However, egg-crates are bulky and take up extra space in the car.

Clothing

Many camping books detail the kind of clothing you should take, and it is a good idea to consult them for complete suggestions. But will your dog need special camping clothes, too?

Most dogs will, of course, bring along the basic fur coat. And for many situations, this is all that is needed. But for extreme weather (hot or cold), or for heavy rain, and for dogs without a lot of fur, you may need to consider a dog sweater or coat. For warmth and comfort, those constructed of fleece are an excellent choice for camping. They are sturdy, wash easily, and provide good protection in dry weather. For hot weather, a terry-cloth sweater can be wetted down to help your dog stay cool. For wet weather, take a parka or rain gear. One company, Classic Cover-Ups, makes a fantastic, lightweight dog parka of Gor-Tex and Hollofil. These are completely waterproof, warm, and almost indestructible (see Appendix H for information on getting dog coats).

Food

Will you need to cook special meals for your dog while you are camping? Only if you do so at home. The basic rule of thumb for feeding dogs while traveling is to give them the same food that they generally eat at home—and in the same quantity. Dogs' digestive systems like consistency, and the last thing your dog needs on a camping trip is an upset stomach or diarrhea. This means that if you cook your dog a special diet of organic vegetables, chicken, and rice at home, you will want to keep it up while camping. If your dog is used to canned food or dry kibble, stick with it while traveling. Of course, adding just a taste of your camp stew to your dog's food probably won't hurt, but keep it to just a taste.

The exception to feeding his usual diet is if you are planning (and have been getting your dog in shape for) a strenuous excursion. Your dog may need extra energy for backpacking, sledding, or skijoring. Talk with your veterinarian about switching to a performance diet if you think that your dog's activity level may merit a different food. You'll need to switch your dog over to the new food a few weeks *before* the trip.

Water

Your dog may need to drink twice as much water or more while camping than he does when hanging around home. If you are going to a place with plenty of drinking water, great. If not, you'll have to bring water.

Some experts recommend that you always start a trip by bringing water from home. The idea is that a dog's digestive system can become upset by new water as well as by different food. If your dog is sensitive, you may do well to heed this advice. One way to get your dog used to water in a new area, and avoid stomach upset, is to bring a gallon of water from home, and as you give your dog water, fill the jug back up with drinking water from your new source. This slowly mixes the home water with the new water. The transition will acclimate your dog.

Many dogs, like many people, can drink water from new places without any problem. If your dog is not sensitive to water changes, just give him the same water that you're drinking.

 Paw Note: *Don't let your dog drink straight from rivers, streams, and other natural water sources. This is a lot easier to say than do! But consider: Dogs are as susceptible to waterborne diseases such as giardia as people. In addition, algae bloom can actually be deadly to dogs. It's best to give your dog filtered or treated water. If you can drink it, it's probably okay for your dog. If you wouldn't drink it, don't let your dog drink it either. (For more on giardia and other water hazards, see Chapter 9.) If you're starting with a puppy, train him not to drink out of natural water sources from a young age. If you have an older dog that is already used to drinking from natural water sources, discourage him by giving him plenty of filtered or treated water. Your dog will be less likely to drink from streams if he's not thirsty.*

Grooming Supplies

To keep yourself looking and feeling your best, you may want a few items such as soap, toothpaste, etc. Your dog will also need a few basic grooming supplies. The basics for your dog are a brush, a flea comb, a towel, and emergency shampoo.

After a fun day of hiking and swimming, your dog, like Minnie, may need a little grooming!
PHOTO COURTESY MARY KROSKE AND JEAN FAIRBANKS

Bring along a brush and comb suitable for your dog's coat—a regular brush for short-haired dogs, and a slicker brush or rake for longer-haired dogs. Fleas, ticks, burrs, mud, and other natural things will find your dog when camping—no doubt about it.

Generally, you can brush, comb, and towel the worst of the earth off your dog, but now and again, you may end up with a surprise and may need to give your dog a good washing. Consider bringing along a dry dog bath (the type in a can that foams on and brushes off). This is available at most pet-supply stores and offers a waterless alternative. If you're taking along a gentle biodegradable soap for yourself, it can double in an emergency for your dog—but check with your veterinarian before you use people shampoo on your dog.

Plastic Bags or Pooper-Scoopers

If you're not wilderness camping, you'll probably have access to an outhouse or bathroom facility. Still, you'll want a way to clean up behind your dog. The plastic-bag method is convenient. Simply slip a bag over your hand like a glove and pick up the poop. Pull the bag off your hand, catching the waste inside. Tie a knot and drop the bag in the nearest can. It does seem a bit ironic to put one of nature's most biodegradable items into one of the least biodegradable containers—the plastic bag. An alternative is a biodegradable bag, which is available from many pet-supply houses. Or, if you are going to be near a trash can, you can use a more traditional pooper-scooper.

For wilderness camping, you'll need to either pack out all waste (human and dog) or bury it. For packing waste, double Ziploc bags will keep that wonderful aroma to a minimum. If you bury waste, do so in cat holes (holes that are six to eight inches deep and at least 200 feet from any water source). Be sure to take a small trowel for digging the cat holes.

Boots

When you think about hiking, blisters, and boots, you usually are thinking about your own feet. But dog paws can suffer, too. Dogs can get sore feet from walking on hot rocks, sand, or dirt and from walking through snow. You can toughen pads up (see Chapter 3), but you may also want to take along a pair of dog boots. Dog boots are great to have along for emergencies. If your dog tears a pad or a nail, a boot can help protect the paw until you can get your dog medical care. Boots for dogs come in all sizes and styles and are available through pet-supply stores and mail-order catalogs (see Appendix H). Here is a breakdown of four common types:

- **Leather.** Leather boots give good protection and good traction, and they last a long time. They are also easy to make yourself. You will have to train your dog to be patient while you put them on, because they lace up.

After a long day's hike, Mattie fell asleep with her boots on.
PHOTO COURTESY PENNY AND MIKE BROZDA

- **Nylon.** Nylon boots are light and tough. They slip on easily and generally use Velcro instead of laces, but they will not hold up as well in rocky terrain.
- **Neoprene.** Boots made from neoprene give good water protection and good insulation from the cold. One brand, Pee Dee's Paw Protectors, is made with a heavy Cordura nylon sole that helps the boots hold up under rougher conditions. They also fasten with Velcro.
- **Polar Fleece.** Polar-fleece boots help keep snow from building up between a dog's toes. They are warm, dry quickly, and usually fasten with Velcro.

Dog Packs

Packs are great for your dog if you are hiking or backpacking. Your dog can help carry supplies and lighten your load. Most dogs love to carry a pack once they get used to it. Dog packs come in all different types from day packs to heavy-duty mountaineering packs. They vary in size from small to extra large. Most dogs heavier than thirty pounds can carry a dog pack, but check with your veterinarian before you have your dog carry a load. Hip dysplasia, back problems, or other health problems may make packing unsafe for a dog. Also, a dog should be well conditioned before he carries a load.

Just how much weight can a dog carry in a pack? Traditional recommendations suggest that dogs carry no more than 25 percent of their body weight in a pack. More recent studies, however, suggest that dogs should carry no more than 10 percent of their body weight. This means that a fifty-pound dog could carry about five pounds. These new recommendations come from studies on service dogs that have carried heavier packs on a daily basis and developed skeletal problems over time.

Realistically, the amount of weight that a dog can carry safely depends on the type of dog, the condition of the dog, how well the pack fits and is loaded, and the physical stress of the trip. Check with your veterinarian and use good judgment when loading up your dog's pack. When in doubt, always err on the side of lighter rather than heavier.

Here are a few tips about dog packs to ensure comfort and safety:

1. The pack needs to fit properly. It should ride high on the dog's shoulders and the straps should be snug but loose enough so that you can stick your finger between the strap and the dog's body. Your dog should be able to move his legs freely, and he should be able to lie down in the "sphinx" position without the pack touching the ground.
2. The pack needs to be balanced. If your dog is carrying his food, for example, divide it into two bags and put one in each side of the pack. Also, pack heavy items near the bottom and lighter items near the top.
3. Always put items that could be damaged by moisture into plastic bags. Dogs seem to get wet even when you don't expect it.

Most dogs love carrying a pack once they are used to it.
PHOTO COURTESY PENNY AND MIKE BROZDA

Teaching Your Dog to Wear a Pack

Spend a little time getting your dog used to the pack before you hit the trail. Here's how to teach your dog to wear a pack:

1. Make the experience fun. The first time you show your dog the pack have a handful of treats in your pocket. Place the empty pack across your dog's back and focus his attention on you. When he stands for a moment with the pack, give him a treat. Then take the pack off and repeat the process. When he stands easily with the pack on his back (for some dogs this happens after two or three times, for others, it takes ten times or more), you can go on to the next step.

2. Fasten the pack securely around your dog and take him for a walk in a safe, comfortable place. This may be around your neighborhood or even in your backyard.

3. When your dog can walk comfortably with the empty pack, start adding light items. Use things that won't move around too much. Increase the weight gradually until your dog can easily carry 10 percent of his body weight.

Other Dog Supplies

- **Tie Out or Crate.** You'll need a place to hook up your dog while you set up camp, cook, and generally do tasks that require your dog to be out of your way. A long leash may work, or you can use any of several different types of cable tie outs. Always supervise your dog while he is on a tie out or long leash. If you are traveling by car, you may want to have a crate for the car and around camp.

> ***Paw Note:*** *Three different types of tie outs are sold for dogs, and all of them pose certain risks if not used properly. A short cable that attaches around a post or tree in a cleared area is the safest. A cable that runs from tree to tree is safe only in cleared areas. A ground stake is okay only if it is secure in the ground and the dog cannot pull it out. All types of tie outs are safe only if they are used in a clear area and where a dog cannot crawl under or on top of anything or get the cable wrapped around anything. Only use tie outs with a flat, buckle-type collar—never with a choke chain, a slip collar, or a pinch collar. Always supervise your dog when he is on a tie out.*

- **Food and Water Bowls.** You can take along your dog's regular food and water bowls, or you can use small plastic bowls. You may want to try the collapsible bowls made specifically for traveling with dogs. For backpackers and hikers, a plastic bag can double as a water or food bowl. Just fold down the sides and fill it with food or water.

- **Extra Collar and Leash.** It never fails that if you don't have an extra collar, your dog will lose his. Thick nylon or leather collars are safest and are less likely to get caught on a branch or brush. Make sure that your extra collar has a set of ID tags. (See Chapter 5 for more about camping ID.) Don't forget the extra leash. A six-foot leash is recommended—it gives your dog a bit of sniffing room but still keeps you in control. If you are traveling light, you can make do in an emergency with a bandanna or short length of rope.

- **Medications.** If your dog needs any medications, be sure to bring enough for the trip. Write down their names and dosages, just in case you lose them in your travels and have to stop at an animal hospital to replace them.

- **Health Certificate, Proof of Vaccinations, and Other Paperwork.** Some parks and camp areas require proof of rabies and other vaccinations before they will let you stay. A rabies certificate or current license may be enough. Call ahead and make sure that you have the necessary paperwork. If you are crossing state or national borders, you may need a health certificate from your veterinarian. This is a certificate which says that your dog is not carrying any communicable diseases. You also may want take any obedience certificates or your dog's Canine Good Citizen certificate. Sometimes having a piece of paper which shows that your dog has been trained can make the difference between being allowed in a camp area or not.

- **Insect Repellent and Sunscreen.** You've probably thought about bringing these items for you—but for your dog? Yes! Mosquitoes, biting flies, and ticks are just a few of the insects that you may encounter on your camping adventure. Think about where you are going, then plan accordingly. Applying a pyrethrin spray or dip before going into flea or tick country can help keep those nasty bugs off your dog. Preventic collars (available from veterinarians) work well to keep ticks from attaching to your dog. Your dog may want a repellent for mosquitoes and other biting insects as well. You may need sunscreen if your dog has very fair skin or pink areas on his nose. Dogs really can sunburn! Talk with your veterinarian about which products will help your dog stay comfortable on your trip.

   A word of caution: Do not use human insect repellent or sunscreen for your dog unless your veterinarian recommends it. Some of the ingredients can be toxic to dogs. Instead, get the type sold at pet-supply stores for use on dogs.

• **Life Jacket.** If you are heading out on a boat, even in calm water, have a life jacket for your dog. Think about your dog being like a small child, and take the same kinds of precautions. You will find several types of life jackets for dogs. When choosing one, look for a proper fit. The jacket should adjust to fit your dog properly. It should be snug enough to

Even in calm water, a life jacket is a good idea.
There are several made just for dogs.
PHOTO BY LARRY MICHAEL; COURTESY DOG DAYS OF WISCONSIN

stay on without being too tight or rubbing. It should fit around the chest without impeding front-leg movement for swimming. It should also keep your dog's head up. Make sure that the life jacket has a grab strap. If your dog falls into the water, you'll want to be able to pull him back into the boat easily. Try to get a life jacket with quick-release straps. They make putting the life jacket on and off easier for everyday use. They are also a good precaution in case you need to get the life jacket off in a hurry.

- **Toys:** Bring along your dog's favorite entertainment—chewies, balls, Frisbees, toys—whatever you think will help him stay happy and occupied. If your dog is a little nervous about traveling, he will be comforted by having a favorite toy or stuffed animal with him.

- **First-Aid Kit.** You'll need a first-aid kit that includes items for both people and dogs. See Chapter 10 for a detailed description.

Bringing along your dog's favorite toys can make hanging out in camp more fun. PHOTO COURTESY MARY KROSKE AND JEAN FAIRBANKS

The Complete Canine Camper Checklist

We consider items with an * to be absolute essentials. The other items should be taken along as appropriate for you and your dog.

- *Shelter (can share yours!)
- *Bedding
- *Food (enough for the trip plus three-day emergency supply)
- *Food and water bowls
- Treats
- *Regular medications (enough for trip plus a three-day emergency supply)
- *Flat collar with camping ID
- Training collar (if applicable)
- *Regular leash
- Long leash, tie out, or crate
- Dog sweater or parka (as needed, depending on conditions and dog)
- Dog pack
- Dog boots (may be included in first-aid supplies)
- *Plastic bags, pooper-scooper, or trowel
- *Dog towel
- *Brush and flea comb
- Soap or shampoo
- *Flea, tick, and other insect repellents
- Sunscreen
- Life jacket (if traveling by boat)
- *Health certificate or proof of vaccinations
- Canine Good Citizen certificate or obedience completion certificate
- Toys and chewies
- *First-aid kit (see Chapter 10)

CHAPTER FIVE

TRAVELING WITH YOUR DOG

Half the fun of going on vacation with your dog is getting to where you are going. Some dogs take to travel like it is second nature, whether that travel be walking, driving, biking, boating, or flying. Other dogs are comfortable with some modes of travel (usually what they are used to) but become uncomfortable with new or different types. A few dogs, however, are so uptight about change that almost any travel is upsetting.

Our dog Jesse loves to travel by car and she is a great companion. She enjoys the view, keeps us company, and makes the trip a lot more fun. Our friends, on the other hand, have a dog that cannot even travel around the block in a car without throwing up. Definitely not fun! But even dogs that become easily upset by change can get used to traveling. Most will even come to love it, because they quickly realize that travel means more time with you. By helping your dog learn to feel comfortable with travel and by taking steps to ensure safety, you and your dog can both head for your camping adventure without becoming stressed in the process.

Traveling By Car

If you have a dog that loves the car and will go anywhere with you anytime, you can probably skip over this next part about getting your dog used to riding in a vehicle. This is for those of you who have puppies or dogs that are not used to car travel, whose dogs are just plain scared of the four-wheeled monster, or whose dogs get carsick.

Getting a dog used to the car is a simple, step-by-step process of desensitization. As with any type of socialization and training, it's easiest if you have a puppy, but even an adult dog can learn to love rides in the car.

First, the don'ts:

- Don't just stick a frightened dog in the car and take off. This can traumatize the dog, and you'll have to spend more time undoing the damage later.
- Don't just take your dog in the car for rides to the veterinarian or kennel. He will quickly learn to hate the car.

Jesse and Blue wait patiently to be buckled in. Some dogs are always ready for a car ride. Others may need training.

- Don't expect your dog to know automatically how to behave in the car. You'll need to teach him the rules and get him used to the sound and feel of a moving car.
- Don't rush the process. Your dog may take several days or several weeks to get used to the car—but once he is, it will be worth the time and effort.
- Remember, your dog's license does not entitle him to actually drive a car.

Now, follow these steps to help an automobile novice learn to love the ride:

1. Have your dog get into the car (use a treat to teach him to jump in) and sit quietly with you for a few moments. Leave the doors open so that he doesn't get worried about being confined. Then take him back out. Repeat this several times. When jumping in and out of the car is no big deal, move on to the next step.

2. Assign your dog a place in the car to call his own. This is particularly important if your dog is frightened or very excitable. He will feel safer and more secure knowing what is expected of him. You may want that spot to be in the back of your station wagon behind a barrier, on the back seat, or in a crate. Put a blanket or towel on the spot to identify his place. When you call your dog into the car, have him now go to his spot, and hang out together for a few minutes with the doors closed. Give him lots of praise and encouragement. Once your dog is comfortable with the doors closed, move on to the next step.

3. Have your dog get into the car and go to his spot. Then start the engine. Let it run for a minute or two and turn it off. Take your dog out of the car. Again, give him lots of praise. When your dog seems comfortable with the engine noise, it's time to go for a ride.

4. Start out with short rides. If your dog gets upset or carsick, you may need to start with only half a block. When your dog can ride comfortably for half a block, increase the distance

to a whole block. Keep increasing the length until you can take a short trip to the beach, park, or another fun place. When you are desensitizing your dog to the car, always make the ride for fun. Your dog will start to associate the car with play and adventure rather than with fear and misery.

5. Once your dog is comfortable with short trips around town, start taking him on longer trips until he is ready to hit the road for a vacation.

6. *Take your time with this process.* Some dogs will be happy travelers after one or two outings, while others may take weeks to become accustomed to the car. The time you spend now will pay off big when you have a companion that is comfortable traveling.

Motion Sickness

Many dogs and almost all puppies become a little motion sick when they first start riding in a car. Some dogs will get over motion sickness as they get used to the ride. Most puppies will outgrow it. Make sure that your dog has plenty of fresh air, doesn't need to go to the bathroom, and hasn't just eaten a big meal.

For most dogs, the desensitization process above should take care of the car sickness, as long as you take it slowly and are careful not to traumatize your dog in the process. This means focusing on the positive, rewarding your dog, and making it seem like traveling in the car will give him the thing he wants most in the world—fun times with you.

If, after you've desensitized your dog to the car, he still has a problem with motion sickness, you may want to talk with your veterinarian. Your dog may have a physical problem that is contributing to the motion sickness. Your veterinarian may also prescribe a medication to prevent motion sickness. Over time, as the dog becomes used to the motion, the medication can be gradually withdrawn.

Paw Note: *Never, never, never leave your dog unattended in the car. If the weather is warm, your dog can suffer from heatstroke even if you leave the windows down and park in the shade. The sun moves and shade quickly becomes sun. And when the temperature is only 75°F, your car can heat up to 120°F in half an hour or less! Dogs can die in that kind of heat. Cold is equally problematic. Your car can become a refrigerator in a matter of minutes. Also, pet thefts from cars are more and more common all the time.*

A Word About Windows

While fresh air is important for your dog's comfort, it's best not to let your dog hang his head out the window. A window open far enough for your dog to hang out is also open far enough for him to jump out or fall out. The wind from a car traveling at forty or fifty miles per hour can hurl dirt, bugs, and rocks into your dog's eyes and cause serious damage. Also, the wind can hurt your dog's ears. Keep the window rolled up enough so that your dog can comfortably and safely enjoy the fresh air.

Seat Belts, Barriers, and Crates

Dog experts disagree on the safest way for a dog to ride in the car. Some say that dogs should always be in a crate or kennel. Others say that a barrier between the front and back of the car is enough. Some recommend seat belts. Although some people think that dogs should remain loose in the car, most experts agree that this practice is the least safe.

We think that it's best to have a dog restrained in one way or another. That way, the dog can't jump in your lap when you're driving and cause an accident, or dash out of the car door unexpectedly and get hit by a passing car. Even well-trained dogs will occasionally become overexcited, and in a car, that could be very dangerous. In an accident, if your dog is restrained, emergency workers can help you both without risk of your dog biting or escaping. Choosing a restraint depends on your dog, your car, and your comfort level.

Car Safety Belts

You can use your car's safety belts on your dog by purchasing a special harness. One type is a harness through which you loop a people seatbelt. It is pretty easy to use and is available at most pet-supply stores. Another option is to fasten a short lead to your dog's regular harness and put the handle loop through the seat belt. Dogs (like children) are much safer when they ride in the back seat of the car.

Barriers

You can obtain a car barrier that blocks the back of a van or station wagon. Some are metal, and some are made of netting. They will keep your dog off your seats and out of your way while still giving him room to move freely. This is great for avoiding mud all over the car but not as good if you want to load up the back with camping supplies.

Crates

Crates or kennels give your dog the most protection in case of an accident. They also keep your dog contained while you drive, protect him from the shifting load of camping gear if you have to stop suddenly, and give you a dog house for your destination. Dogs need to be carefully trained to the crate so that they experience it as a safe home rather than as a cage.

How to Crate Train Your Dog
1. Place the crate in a well-used area of the house. Put in a comfy blanket or towel and a few of your dog's toys. Let your dog sniff and investigate the crate on his own. Leave the door open to let your dog investigate.
2. When your dog seems comfortable with the crate, take a favorite treat and toss it into the crate, saying your dog's

Paw Note: *Crates must be used humanely. They are not designed to be a cage. They are meant to replicate a comfortable, cozy den. The crate must be big enough to allow your dog to stand up and turn around. The floor should be padded, especially when traveling in a bumpy car. Give your dog lots of breaks for stretching, exercise, and water. Don't leave your dog in a crate for long periods of time. Carefully train your dog to the crate so that he is comfortable and happy when he must be confined.*

name, followed by, "Crate." Let your dog go into the crate and come immediately back out. Praise your dog as he goes in. Do this several times until your dog is comfortable going in and out of the crate.

3. Try feeding your dog in the crate a few times. This will encourage a positive association. When your dog seems comfortable with going in and out of the crate, start feeding him in his regular place again.

4. When your dog goes into the crate easily, start closing the door for just a few minutes. Continue rewarding your dog with a treat and praise. Slowly extend the time your dog stays in the crate, adding a few minutes at a time.

5. Remain nearby while your dog is getting used to being in the crate. When your dog settles into the crate comfortably for half an hour or so, start leaving him alone for a few minutes at a time.

6. Don't let your dog out of the crate when he is whining or barking. Wait until he settles down to let him out.

7. Go slowly when crate training your dog. If you take your time, your dog will become comfortable and will begin to see the crate as his own private space.

8. Leave the crate in a place where you hang out. Keep the door open when you're not confining your dog. Most dogs will use the crate as their own special den or bed.

When I first started using crates with my dogs, it was out of desperation. I had had dogs for most of my life and had never had to resort to any type of confinement. But this time I had two puppies that needed to be left unsupervised for a few hours each day. We did not have a safe area inside, and, inside or out, they were collectively destroying our home. I was also very worried about their safety. Couch stuffing could not possibly be part of a healthy diet. I did not like the idea of locking my dogs up, but I was willing to keep them safe.

After several weeks of using crates with the puppies, however, I became a crate convert. It happened one day when I came home from work, let my pups out of their crates, and watched them romp and play for a while. When they were finished with their play, they both went back to their crates and went to sleep. Soon they voluntarily used them for their main rest area.

The puppies outgrew the need for confinement within a few months, but to this day, my dogs love their crates, and I am always grateful when I travel to have a comfy and safe den to take with us.

Truck Tie-Downs

If your dog rides in the back of an open pickup, you will need to have a restraint or tie-down for safety. In some areas, pickup restraints are required by law. You can make one yourself by bolting a hook to the center of the truck bed right behind the cab and attaching a short, sturdy leash to a harness or flat collar. Or you can purchase a similar item that hooks a line to the tie-downs on each corner near the cab. Both devices keep the dog from jumping or falling out of the truck. Another, fancier restraint called the Leash O' Life attaches a track with a cable to the bed of the truck. This allows a dog to move back and forth but limits side-to-side movement so that the dog cannot jump or fall from the truck.

Packing Woes

When you are packing your car for a trip, it is essential that you take your dog's needs into account. You will be jamming

Paw Note: *Improperly restrained dogs in open pickup-truck beds can be seriously injured if they try to jump out or if you are in an accident. Never attach the restraint to a choke or prong collar. If you are using a flat collar, make sure that it fits tightly enough so that it cannot be pulled over the dog's head. No part of your dog's body should reach over the side of the truck bed at any time. If you are using a commercial restraint, always follow manufacturer recommendations.*

sleeping bags, coolers, tents, fishing gear, barbecues, and more into a space not meant to hold so much. While there are many ways to pack a vehicle, you will always have to allow your dog room for comfort and safety. Be sure that your dog has enough space to stand up, turn around, and lie down. Also, make sure that the load cannot shift and that camping gear will not fall on your dog.

Canoes, Kayaks, and Rafts

If you are lucky, your dog may take to riding in a boat like he was born for the sole purpose of exploring waterways. But most of us have dogs that are either timid around boats or too rambunctious. Getting these dogs used to riding in the confined area of a canoe, kayak, or raft will take special training.

Get your dog accustomed to your alternative mode of transportation much the way you get him used to traveling in a car. Start slowly, take your time, and make it fun. The following suggestions are specifically for a canoe but can be adapted for a kayak or raft:

1. Make sure that your dog knows the sit, down, and stay commands. You'll need these if your dog starts to move around in the boat when you are on the water.

Most dogs can learn to ride safely in a kayak or canoe.
PHOTO COURTESY MARY KROSKE AND JEAN FAIRBANKS

2. Start on dry land a few weeks before your planned trip. Put an old Ensolite pad or some other nonslip pad in the bottom of the boat. Let your dog check out the canoe and see you getting in and out of it.

3. Have your dog get into and out of the canoe a few times. Use a treat if necessary to help him learn to jump in and out. If you have a smaller dog or a dog that cannot easily jump in and out, you may want to lift him in and out of the boat.

4. Once your dog is used to getting in and out of the boat, have him jump in and sit or lie down. Teach him where he is supposed to be. Make the experience fun and give him lots of praise.

5. When your dog is comfortable in the canoe on land, it's time to head for the water. Make sure that your dog is wearing a life jacket, then push off. Make your first excursion short and fun. Slowly lengthen your trips, but do not push your dog's comfort level.

6. It may take one or two overturned canoes until your dog learns not to move around too much—and you learn to counterbalance his weight. Don't get frustrated—just be prepared and practice in a safe area.

7. Before you head out on a longer trip, exercise your dog well because he will be hanging out quietly in the canoe while you are paddling. Take lots of breaks to let your dog stretch and move around.

Some people worry about taking a dog that is afraid of the water out on a boat. Just be sure that your dog can swim before you embark on a boating trip (see Chapter 7 for how to teach your dog to swim). Ironically, dogs that love the water usually cause more problems than dogs that hate it. Water-loving dogs are more likely to jump out of the boat to swim after a duck or fish, or just to cool off. For dogs that really like the water, you'll have to be extra clear on the rules regarding when, where, and how the boat is to be exited.

Safety Tips

• Teach your dog to swim and always have him wear a life jacket. Even under calm conditions, a dog that accidentally falls into the water can get hurt.

• Remember how easy it is to tip a canoe if you shift your weight too fast? Your dog's weight shifting can also tip the canoe. Make sure that he is well trained. If your dog moves fast and risks tipping the boat, brace yourself by assuming a stable, kneeling position.

• Do not take your dog out under rough conditions—whitewater rafting is not a good idea with a dog. When you judge the conditions, ask yourself if they would be safe for a small child. If so, then they are probably safe for your dog. If not, leave your dog at home.

• Protect your dog from the heat and sun. A dog riding on the water in warm weather can easily become overheated. Give him plenty of water and take breaks to cool off. You can also help your dog stay cool by wetting him down or rigging up

Is this what they mean by dog paddling?

shade in the boat. If you need a hat and sunglasses, your dog will need protection, too.

- Your dog may also need protection if you are traveling in very cold conditions. You can use dog boots, polar-fleece coats, or even a wetsuit to help your dog stay warmer. (Custom wetsuits for dogs are made by O'Neil Wetsuits in Santa Cruz, California.) Keeping your dog protected from wind can also help.

- Watch for rough terrain on the shore. For example, oyster shells on the beach can rip into a dog's pads. If the shore is rough with sharp shells or the sand is particularly hot, have your dog wear boots.

> **Paw Note:** *Before deciding to travel by boat or bike with your dog, ask yourself, "What is in it for him?" Remember, you will be asking your dog to sit or lie quietly for long periods of time—something that is unnatural for a dog. What will the payoff be? Will you be spending fun times hiking and playing once you reach your destination? If not, consider leaving your dog at home or planning a different type of trip.*

Traveling by Bike

For the die-hard bicycler with a small dog, bicycle touring can be an ideal form of getting around—and of traveling to different camping areas. Whether your dog will be riding in a carrier on the back of your bike or in a cart pulled behind your bike, you will need to teach him to ride quietly. As with traveling by boat, your dog will do better if you give him lots of exercise before starting out.

To teach your dog to ride safely in an open carrier or cart, follow these steps:

1. Get your dog used to wearing a harness.
2. If you are using a carrier, you will need to lift your dog into the carrier and buckle him in. Begin by simply putting him in the carrier, buckling him in, and taking him out. With a cart, you will be able to teach your dog to jump in and out himself.
3. After your dog is used to getting in and out of the carrier or trailer, take very short rides. Gradually increase the distance until your dog is comfortable with longer rides.

A child's cart can be adapted for a small dog.

Safety Tips

- Make sure that your dog is comfortable in the carrier or cart before you take him into traffic.
- You will need to consider weather conditions and make sure that your dog is neither too hot nor too cold. Provide shade and plenty of water in hot weather. Provide a sweater and warm blankets in colder weather.
- A cover for protection from sun, wind, and rain is essential. Carts come with a cover. If you make a carrier, you will need to incorporate a cover into your design.

Paw Note: *A local veterinarian told us about a carrier that she helped a client design for a bicycle trip across country. They attached a platform to the rack on the back of the bicycle, then attached an airline-approved pet carrier to the platform frame with specially made clamps similar to those used to hold down car batteries. The animal riding in the crate (a cat in this case) did not have to be buckled in because the carrier was covered. When the bicyclist stopped, she could easily remove the crate and take it with her to campgrounds or motels. In case of an accident, the animal was fully enclosed in very strong plastic and was well protected.*

Trains, Planes, Boats, and Buses

Using public transportation to travel with your dog is not a very good option, especially in the United States. Most trains, buses, and cruise ships don't allow dogs, with the exception of assistance dogs. In other countries, the acceptance of dogs on public transportation varies greatly. Call ahead and ask about traveling with your dog if you are considering using public transportation.

The one exception to the "no-public-transport-with-dogs" rule is traveling by airplane. Many commercial airlines do allow dogs, but there is some controversy about whether flying with dogs is safe.

To Fly or Not to Fly

You have two options when you travel with your dog by plane. If you have a dog that is small enough to fit inside a carrier that will slide under the seat, you can take your dog on board with you. If you have a larger dog, he will need to travel in the cargo hold.

Many people are concerned about the safety of dogs traveling in the cargo hold. It used to be that dogs were sometimes placed in cargo holds without proper ventilation, temperature control, lighting, and pressure. But stricter regulations and enforcement, as well as a lot of bad press for the airlines, have been a conduit for safer flying conditions for dogs. Still, safety records are inconsistent and certain conditions can make flying riskier for your dog. Here are a few suggestions to help ensure that your dog travels safely:

- Book your reservations early on a nonstop flight. Fewer takeoffs and landings and no plane changes mean fewer risks.
- Get a list of requirements from the airline. Make sure that your crate meets the airline's size and safety requirements and is well labeled. Include emergency contacts at both your home and your destination. Include an authorization for emergency veterinary care.
- Make sure that your dog has a physical exam before flying. Most airlines require a health certificate within ten days of travel.
- Avoid traveling during hot or cold times of the year. If you are traveling when the temperature may be hot, book flights for early or late in the day. If you are traveling when the temperature may be cold, book flights for the middle of the day.

- Allow plenty of time for check-in. Watch through the window at the gate and make sure that your dog is boarded on the plane before you board. Ask the airline representative at the gate to talk directly with the baggage handlers to confirm that the dog has been loaded onto the plane.
- Give your dog water thirty to sixty minutes before the flight, and give him a chance to urinate. Be sure that your dog has water in the crate while flying, but use caution—water in a crate can spill, making your dog uncomfortable or cold. Use a plastic bowl with a hole in the top, and freeze the whole bowl of water ahead of time. Your dog will be able to drink small amounts as the water melts. Also, use the little water cup that comes with the crate. It is inadequate by itself but can be refilled easily by airline personnel without opening the crate if your flight is delayed.
- Don't tranquilize your dog unless absolutely necessary. Experts agree that the risks of tranquilizing a dog for a flight are greater than the benefits *in most cases*. If your dog reacts negatively to the tranquilizer while in the air, no one will be there to help. If you must tranquilize your dog, talk with your veterinarian about the right dose, and test the medication before flying.
- Do not feed your dog for six to eight hours before the flight. Make sure that your dog gets plenty of exercise before flying. Also, have your dog relieve himself right before he is checked onto the plane.
- Do not fly with very young dogs (less than eight weeks of age), very old dogs, dogs with health problems, or dogs with pug noses. Pug-nose dogs like Bulldogs, Pugs, Boston Terriers, and Pekingese can have trouble breathing on airplanes.

Crossing Borders

To cross state or national borders, you will need health certificates and proof of current rabies vaccinations. Many campgrounds and parks require these as well. You will need to call ahead and find out how many days prior to crossing the border the certificate may be dated and what it needs to include.

Certificates usually need to be dated no more than ten to thirty days prior to border crossings.

Also, ask about quarantines or other special regulations when traveling across borders. For example, Hawaii has a 120-day quarantine for dogs. Great Britain has a 180-day quarantine. When traveling to Mexico with a dog, you need to take an International Certificate of Vaccination to a consulate prior to crossing the border. Rules and regulations about traveling with dogs change regularly, so you'll want to get the latest information before making your travel plans. To find information for travel in foreign countries, contact the consulate or office of tourism for the country in which you plan to travel.

ID and Other "Just-In-Case" Tips

Unexpected things can happen when you travel with your dog. You may not want to think about you or your dog getting lost or hurt, but it is possible. You will be able to travel with greater security knowing that you are well prepared for emergencies. Follow these suggestions so that you will be ready for the unexpected.

- Make sure that your dog has a well-fitting collar with an ID. You may want to have a nameplate that attaches directly to your dog's collar with rivets. Because this sits flat against the collar, it is less likely to get lost while hiking or exploring.
- If you are away from home, you may want another set of ID tags that has the name, address, and phone number of a friend or relative to contact if you cannot be reached. You can do this by having a separate collar and tags just for traveling.
- Consider having an additional tag on your dog's collar that says: "THIS DOG IS LOST. REWARD" on one side and, "OBTAIN EMERGENCY VETERINARY CARE—EXPENSES WILL BE PAID" on the other side.
- Consider having your veterinarian implant a microchip on your dog with your name, address, and phone number. Animal shelters and veterinarians with scanners can identify your dog even if he loses his collar.

- Consider having your dog tattooed with a unique identifying number or code and list it with a national registry.
- Keep your dog close to you and on a leash anytime the weather or other conditions may upset him, especially during storms or in high winds.
- Write down the names and dosages of any medications your dog is taking. It is handy to have this information written down in case the medication gets lost.
- Keep an information sheet in the glove compartment of your car with emergency information for your dog. Include his name and any special needs. Also include names of people to contact if you are injured and cannot care for him.

Teaching Your Dog to Eliminate on Command

One of the best things you can teach your dog is to pee and poop on command. Impossible, you say. Dogs do it when they are good and ready, when they find the right spot, and when they need to, but not when you want them to. Well, that's exactly what I said when my training instructor suggested that all of us in puppy class do this. But I was working hard to be an A-plus student, so I tried it. And guess what? Not only can you easily teach a dog to do his business on command, it is wonderfully convenient when you are traveling and you hit the rest stop. You can lead your dog to the proper area, have him "get busy," and be on your way. Here's how:

1. Pick a word or command. "Get busy" works well, but you can use any words that you want.
2. For about a week, every time you see your dog about to pee or poop, say, "Get busy" (or your command word) with enthusiasm. As soon as he is finished, say, "Good, get busy." Before you know it, your dog will associate the word with the act.
3. Now start trying it out in different places when you know he is about to do it. Don't forget the praise.
4. Once your dog has associated the word with the action in different areas, you'll be ready to use it as a command. This process takes anywhere from a week to a month to teach, depending on the dog.

Before You Leave Home

You've made your list, bought your supplies, and called ahead to the camp area. Your dog is in shape, and he knows how to ride in a car, canoe, or bike carrier. Just a few more things need to be done.

- Clip your dog's nails. Long nails can tear car seats and tent bottoms and can get snagged on rocks. Shorter nails will keep your dog safer and your gear in good shape.
- Clip your dog's fur around nails, under the belly and around the ears, especially on longer-haired dogs. This can help immensely with campsite grooming. You'll be able to locate ticks, foxtails, and burrs much more easily. Don't shave a long-haired dog, however. The fur acts as insulation, protecting the dog from heat, sun, and cold.
- Take steps to prevent flea and tick problems. If you are going into heavy flea and tick country, you will want to either dip your dog with pyrethrin or get him a flea-and-tick collar or a Preventic collar. Talk with your veterinarian about the best flea-and-tick-control method for your dog.

Run, dog, run! At the end of a long day of traveling, make sure there is a payoff for your dog.
PHOTO COURTESY MARY KROSKE AND JEAN FAIRBANKS

CHAPTER SIX

TRAINING TIPS AND MORE

If you're like most people, your dog is the best, most wonderful creature on earth. Everyone can see how great your dog is just by looking, right? Unfortunately, many people, including a lot of people who camp, don't know about dogs, don't understand dogs, or just plain don't like dogs (can you imagine?). Even people who do like dogs may not be happy about a dog that poses a serious danger to wildlife or that disturbs the peace and quiet. And if your dog is unruly or out of control, even *you* may not be happy with him. That's where the Canine Good Camper comes in.

The Canine Good Camper

The goal of the Canine Good Citizen (CGC) program, sponsored by the American Kennel Club (AKC) is to encourage dog owners to socialize and train their dogs to be responsible members of society. It provides testing and certification to both purebred and mixed-breed dogs. A Canine Good Citizen certificate, showing that your dog has passed the basic test, is now recognized as the standard for basic dog behavior.

The Canine Good Camper is our own version of this program, with the sole purpose of helping *you* and *your dog* become good citizen campers. Notice the emphasis on "you" and "your dog." You are as important a piece of this program as your dog.

There are two reasons for introducing the Canine Good Camper program. The first is out of respect and concern for wild lands. These guidelines will help minimize the impact of camping with dogs on wilderness areas. The less the natural environment is disturbed, the more the wild areas will be preserved for future visits by you, your kids, and your grandchildren. The second is to ensure continued access to camping with dogs. Many places no longer allow dogs. The best way to keep areas open to dogs is by acting conscientiously.

> *Paw Note: The Canine Good Camper is not recognized by any national dog organizations, nor is there an official test. But by following the guidelines of the Canine Good Camper, you will be helping to preserve camp areas for the future enjoyment of both people and dogs, protect natural resources, and ensure yourself a great camping experience. We do recommend that you train your dog for the AKC's Canine Good Citizen program and get tested and certified. Not only will you and your dog have a great set of skills for everyday situations, but many motels and other public areas are more likely to accept your dog if he has passed the test and you have the certificate to prove it.*

Your Part

The following eight steps outline your role in being a Canine Good Camper:

1. **Socialize your dog.** A well-socialized dog will react in a confident and calm manner toward other dogs, people, and

A well-socialized dog is able to accept other creatures.

wildlife. Ideally, you will socialize your dog as a puppy, but even an older dog can learn to stay calm around others. Dogs with good early socialization will be the easiest to get ready for a camping trip. They will simply need to be exposed slowly to new situations until their confidence builds. But even if you have a dog that is difficult, don't despair. Socialization training isn't tough—it just takes time and patience.

When I first got my dog, Charlie, he was two years old and extremely shy—so shy that he would not let a new person touch him for two to three weeks. Whenever a person walked down the street, he would dart in the other direction. He was insecure on leash and worse off leash. But after a few years of very slow and careful socialization, Charlie became a calm and easygoing dog. He was always a little shy, but he learned to trust people and he became confident in most situations.

To socialize your dog, you will need to do basic training and then expose your dog to all different types of situations. Take him on walks. Take him around kids. Take him around other animals. The more situations dogs are exposed to, the less likely they are to act out in new situations.

2. **Follow the rules.** Camping areas have different rules and regulations for dogs. Most places have leash and voice-control requirements. Some have rules about where your dog should sleep and policies about cleaning up after your canine companion. *It is essential that you follow the rules of the area you are visiting at all times.* If you want the rules to be different, talk to the people in charge, write letters, and work to change them. But while they are in effect, respect and follow them or you may find that dogs are not allowed at all the next time you visit.

3. **Keep your dog under control.** This means having your dog on a leash or under excellent voice control at all times, teaching your dog to remain quiet and calm when appropriate, being able to settle your dog down in unsettling situations, and being able to regain control if your dog becomes too excited. Again, basic obedience and leadership will help you keep your dog under control. Equally important is your ability to know what will set your dog off so that you can avoid trouble. For example, if you have a dog that will chase after ducks, it's your job to see the ducks before he does and have a tight hold on his leash.

4. **Use a leash.** Always keep your dog on a leash when the rules require it. If you are in an area where dogs are allowed off leash—and your dog is under voice control—use good judgment about when and where you let your dog romp and run and enjoy freedom. *Only do so when you can pay attention and supervise.* The wilderness is home to many plants and animals. A leash will help you keep your dog on the trail so that he doesn't trample fragile plants, and it will keep him from disrupting wildlife. Using a leash

Your dog can be trained to love his leash.

If your dog is off leash, make sure that he is under good voice control.

can also keep your dog safe and out of harm's way. On hikes or long walks, it will keep him from exhausting himself (you've seen those dogs that run up and down the trail, covering five miles for every one the person walks). It will allow you the luxury of relaxing and knowing that your dog is safe.

5. **Always clean up after your dog.** If you are in a more populated area, you will need to clean up behind your dog so that other people and animals won't have to deal with your dog's waste. Even the most fanatical dog lover hates to step in dog poop. If you are in a remote area, you will need to clean up after your dog so that you won't be disrupting the balance of nature.

Ruffing it responsibly means cleaning up behind you-know-who.

6. **Follow trail and camp etiquette.** When you meet others on the trail, move off to the side. Don't let your dog (no matter how friendly he is) run up to strangers on the trail. If you encounter horses or other large animals on the trail, move off to the side and give them plenty of space. Many horses are easily spooked around dogs. If you are in a camp area or on a trail, keep your dog close to you. Don't let your dog wander through other people's campsites.

7. **Accept responsibility.** Imagine that the worst has happened. Somehow your dog escaped from his leash—perhaps it broke—and he ran into the neighboring campsite, lifted his leg on their tent, ripped open their pack and ate their dinner, and then, when the neighbors returned to camp, he growled menacingly. (Where were you when all of this was going on? Taking a nap nearby, perhaps, believing that your dog was securely tied out.) Never shirk responsibility for your dog's actions, no matter how big or how small the infringement may seem to you. Apologize, apologize, and apologize some more. Offer to pay for damage, cleaning, etc.

   Most important, if your dog barks at a person or in any other way appears menacing, never say, "Don't worry—he doesn't bite." It doesn't matter if your dog would really bite or not. The person at the receiving end of a barking dog is acting reasonably if he is scared. If you say, "Don't worry," you are insulting the person's intelligence. Instead of saying, "My dog doesn't bite," get your dog under control immediately and then apologize.

8. **Make the trip worth it for your dog.** This is the most important step. Traveling can be stressful for dogs, and they are often expected to contain their most basic instincts (such as chasing wildlife, rolling in smelly things, and playing wildly). Keep your trip dog-focused, and make sure that your dog has time to play and that the payoff is worth the work. In other words, don't expect your dog to ride in a car all day, get into camp, and immediately settle down and then wait in camp for you the next day while you fish. Walk, hike, and play with your dog. You'll both have more fun.

Your Dog's Part

Your dog needs to work hard to learn good camping manners. Here are the things your dog should be able to do before you head out on a camping trip.

1. **Be respectful of people and other animals.** Your dog should be able to see other people and dogs and accept their presence in a quiet and friendly manner. Like the first step in the "Your Part" section of the Canine Good Camper, this is about socialization. You will have to socialize your dog according to his natural tendencies.

   For example, a dog that loves everyone will have to learn not to bother people and other animals in camp. A dog that is protective will have to stay calm when he is approached by other campers. A dog with a high prey drive will need to control his instincts around wild animals. Again, don't despair if your dog has a hard time with any of these situations. With your help, he can learn to accept most circumstances confidently.

   When Melanee first got her dog, Jesse was only about four months old, but she was already a handful. She was very excitable and often jumped uncontrollably on people. Around other dogs, she was aggressive. With cats and other animals, she went into a high-pitched, prey-drive whine that made neighbors come out to see if she was all right. It was obvious that Jesse had not been well socialized as a younger pup. Today, with lots of training, she is now able to stay calm around people, get along with most dogs, and control her prey-drive yelping.

2. **Accept a leash.** All dogs that are taken into public areas including parks, forests, and wilderness areas need to be able to walk on a leash. To help accomplish this, keep your dog leashed when you are out for fun times as well as when you simply want control. Then you and your dog will both associate the leash with fun and good times together. Whether your dog walks in front of you, behind you, or next to you is your choice, but he should learn to walk without pulling.

3. **Come when called.** This is probably the most important thing for all camping dogs to know. Even if you are planning to keep your dog on a leash your entire trip, you could lose your grip or the leash may break. Having your dog return when you call is essential. It can save your dog's life if he starts to run toward a rattlesnake, it can save the life of the rabbit he is chasing, it can keep him from getting lost in the woods, and it can save you from having to chase an out-of-control dog around the campsite.

4. **Hang out calmly in camp.** Your dog will need to be able to settle quietly in camp. For some dogs, this is easy. Others will need to be taught to hang out. If you have a dog with a lot of energy, exercise usually helps. For all dogs, a comfortable spot in the shade where they can simply relax will help.

5. **Remain quiet in camp.** Dogs that bark continuously while camping are usually frightened or nervous. A confident and comfortable dog is usually quiet. Your dog knowing and responding to a "quiet" command can help. But socializing your dog will help the most. If your dog is protective by nature, teach him to bark only when he senses a real threat.

6. **Down and stay on command.** Down asks your dog to lie down immediately. It is a great command for every dog to know. When a dog lies down on command, he is respecting you as the leader and disengaging from other activities. When combined with the stay, a down command can be a lifesaver in an emergency. It's also helpful for everyday camping needs. For example, if you are camped at a place with outhouses, you can have your dog down and stay while you use the facilities.

Once when I was out walking with our two dogs, a young child came tearing down the path on a bike. He fell hard not far from where we were walking and began screaming. I put both dogs on a down stay and left them to

*Your dog will need
to be able to settle
quietly in camp.*
PHOTO COURTESY
PENNY AND MIKE
BROZDA

help the child. Fortunately, the boy suffered only a few
scrapes. Equally as fortunate, I could depend on my dogs to
wait calmly and reliably while I helped out.

7. **Adjust well to new and different situations.** Dogs that
   camp will have to accept changing weather, schedules, terrain, sleeping arrangements, and more. They may see animals and plants that are new. They will have to adapt if
   your car breaks down on the way or if you get caught in a
   thunderstorm. You get the idea. Again, this is a socialization
   process. The more your dog gets out and about before camping, the easier he will adjust to changes when camping.

Even if you love your dog's voice, your wilderness neighbors may not enjoy his serenade.

8. **Respect your leadership.** Dogs need leadership. They are pack animals and all dog packs, wild and domestic, have a leader. They need to know that someone is ultimately in charge. You have to be the pack leader to maintain order, especially when you are traveling to new places. Your dog will not always know what to expect and will need to look to you for guidance and be willing to follow your lead.

A Few More Thoughts about Instincts, Drives, and Socialization

We have a good friend, Kathy, who works with dogs and has nine of her own. She is constantly reminding us that no matter how well a dog is trained and socialized, "dogs will always be dogs." What this means for campers with canines is that you must always expect—no matter how well trained your dog is—that instinct could kick in at any time.

The Good Canine Camper section talked a lot about socialization and training. Some people see socialization as training your dog to behave. But socialization is really a process of learning your dog's instincts, respecting them, and working with them. Training is just one piece of that process.

For example, one of our dogs has a very high prey drive—higher than any dog I have ever known. And, because of her prey drive, no matter how well trained she is, she may never really be safe off leash in the wilderness. Her instincts could make her follow a scent into danger, not to mention the risk to wildlife. It is equally important to remember that while dogs like Jesse have wild-predator instincts, they don't have wild-animal survival skills.

Recognizing your dog's drives—prey, protection, and pack— can help you shape your training program.

In order to train your dog effectively for camping, you'll need to recognize your dog's instinctive drives. Consider his prey drive, protection drive, and pack drive.

Prey drive is that part of a dog's instinct that literally drives the dog to hunt. This type of behavior becomes apparent when your dog chases cats or balls, shakes toys, and is motivated by food. If your dog has a high prey drive, you will need to keep him carefully controlled around wildlife.

Protection drive is the part of a dog that makes him either fight or flee in threatening situations. Is your dog more likely to fight when he is threatened, or will he roll over and bare his belly? If your dog is strong on fighting it is important that he listen to you. If your dog is more likely to flee, you'll need to let him know that you will stay in charge. If your dog has a high protection drive—either fight or flight—keep him near you and let him know that you are the leader.

Pack drive is the part of a dog that determines how much he responds to leadership. A dog with a high pack drive needs you to be a strong leader or he will have to do the job himself. If your dog becomes the leader, you can count on problems. To place yourself in the leadership role, you don't need to be aggressive or dominant—you simply need to act in a way that will assert yourself as the pack leader. Here is how you can help your dog see you as leader:

- Eat first, then feed your dog. In a wild dog pack, the top dog always eats first.
- Walk ahead of your dog, rather than following his lead.
- When you play games like tug-of-war, make sure that you "win" more often than your dog. Always end the game with yourself as the "winner." Top dogs always win.
- If your dog paws, nudges, or whines for attention, ignore him. This is a way of indirectly challenging your leadership.
- Ask your dog to sit before you pet him. This reinforces your role as the leader; your dog has to do something for you before you do something for him.

- Spend a few minutes a day doing basic training. Your dog will love the attention, and you will have more overall control. You also will be reinforcing yourself as leader.

All different types of dogs with diverse personalities and instincts can become great campers. Charlie, who was forever uncomfortable around people, loved the wilderness and was an ever-enduring hiker. Jesse—whose instincts drive her to hunt and force us to keep her on leash—is the type of camper that sees and hears everything. We always feel safe and protected in her presence. Blue doesn't have an ounce of protection drive, but she is always ready to play. She reminds us after a hard day of travel or hiking that we are really there just to have fun. Small dogs, big dogs, shy dogs, wild dogs, playful dogs, and serious dogs can all become fabulous camping companions.

Training Tips for Camping Companions

So how do you train your dog to do his part? Training is a long-term process and takes commitment on your part. The suggestions here will get you started.

- Make teaching your dog fun. Focus on what your dog does right instead of what he does wrong. You'll enjoy it more, and so will your dog.
- Use motivation to teach your dog new things. The motivation can be food, a toy, or lavish praise.
- Timing is critical in training. The second your dog does what you want, give him lots of praise.
- Using food to teach your dog new things is great, but don't depend on it forever. When your dog really knows something, start phasing out the food and replacing it with praise.
- When you ask your dog to do something, start by saying his name to get his attention, then follow with the command. For example, "Jesse, come!"
- Don't repeat commands. If the dog doesn't respond, show him what to do.

- Never hit or scold your dog when training. Training equals teaching, and dogs, like people, learn best with positive reinforcement.
- If you and your dog are having a hard time with something, try a new approach. Different dogs learn in different ways.
- Never work with your dog when you are mad.
- Dogs learn fastest when you work in short blocks of time more often. It's better to do a little every day—say five to ten minutes at a time—than an hour or two once a week.
- Consistency is the key to dog training. The more consistent you are, the faster your dog will learn.

Find a Training Method that Works for You

There are many different styles of dog training. Some are based on motivation and some on correction, and others work with a combination of the two. The most important part of training is *you,* which means that you need to choose a method that works with *your* personality.

Motivational training works primarily on rewarding the behavior you want and ignoring the behavior you don't want. Correctional training works by correcting a dog that is not doing what you want, usually with a training collar. Combination training rewards positive behavior and corrects negative behavior. Most dog trainers use a combination technique, but some lean more heavily one way or the other. You are more likely to follow through if you use a training method that feels right to you.

Do you have to go to a class to train your dog? No—definitely not. Some people instinctively train their dogs without ever taking them to a class or even doing formal exercises. Other people can learn about training from books or videos. You can also hire a private trainer to help you. Taking a class can be helpful, however, especially with socialization. A class will help you teach your dog and will give your dog exposure to other dogs.

Finding a Dog-Training Class That Works For You

- *Find a class that fits your schedule and budget.* If you choose a dog class that is too expensive or isn't convenient, you will be a lot less likely to follow through.
- *Ask the instructor about the training methods used in class.* Listen carefully as he or she describes the training methods. If you like the approach, you will probably like the class.
- *Ask the instructor if he or she has time in class or outside of class to answer questions or deal with individual problems.* While teachers can't give all of the class time or attention to any one student, they should be available for consultation about specific problems.
- *Watch a class.* You can learn a lot about the instructor's style of training by watching a class. Do the dogs in the class seem to be having fun? Are they engaged with their people? Don't worry about one shy dog or a dog that seems to be scared. Pay attention to the general atmosphere.

There is nothing worse on a camping trip than having your dog be out of control—or in control of you. Camping presents all kinds of new and exciting adventures for both dogs and people. Basic training and socializing will help you stay in charge, ensuring your dog's safety, respect for the wilderness, and your own sanity!

Taking the time now for training will ensure a relaxing, enjoyable trip.
PHOTO COURTESY PENNY AND MIKE BROZDA

CHAPTER SEVEN

FUN ACTIVITIES FOR YOU AND YOUR DOG

By this time, you may be thinking, "My goodness, look at all we have to do to prepare for camping. Look at how much my dog needs to know, and all we need to take. Look at all the responsibility. Is it really worth it?" The answer to that is a 100-percent yes! Camping is fun, and spending time with your dog is fun. When you combine the two, the fun simply multiplies. Now is the time to get down to the business of having a good time with your dog. Here are our favorite camping activities, with tips on how to make the most of them.

Hiking

If you spend your time in the company of a dog, you're probably used to walking—long walks, short walks, walks for potty stops, walks for exercise, walks to relieve boredom, and walks for walking's sake. So what's the difference between walking and hiking? In practical application, not much, but in attitude, everything. Think of a walk as a comfortable outing down a

When hiking, your dog's' senses can cue you into sights and sounds that you may have otherwise missed.

well-traveled lane. Think of a hike as an adventure. Hiking is rugged. Hiking is outdoorsy. Hiking is the wilderness experience. It means leaving the mainstay of human existence and paying a visit to your wild friends. You can hike in the desert or mountains, near beaches or waterfalls, close to the city, or deep in the wilderness. Hiking with dogs offers rewards beyond explanation. Just try it, and you'll see what we mean.

I've heard people suggest that hiking with a dog simply scares off the wildlife, meaning you'll see and hear less. Actually, hiking with a dog that is under control, either on leash or well trained to stay nearby, will do just the opposite. Early one morning while out hiking, Melanee noticed Jesse's ears perk up. She followed Jesse's line of sight and spotted a coyote just before it headed over the crest of the hill. Without Jesse along, she probably would have missed seeing that beautiful creature. Dogs have fabulous senses of hearing and smell. When you are hiking, their senses can cue you into sights and sounds that you may otherwise miss.

Getting Ready for Hiking

The following steps will ensure that you have a great time hiking:

1. **Have your dog well socialized and leash trained.** If you have any doubts about whether your dog is ready for hiking, review Chapter 6. It's better to be ready than to take a dog that will be overly stressed.

2. **Choose a hike that meets your abilities and those of your dog.** Don't try to go too far or climb too high if you or your dog are not up to the challenge. Think about the kind of shape you are both in and how adapted you are to the altitude, the temperature, and the terrain.

3. **Protect your feet.** This goes for both you and your dog. You need to wear hiking shoes that are comfortable and broken in and that offer good support. Trim your dog's nails about a week before hiking. Newly trimmed nails can be a little tender, and long nails can be a hazard. Don't forget the dewclaws. These nails have a way of tearing out at the most inopportune moments. If your dog has soft paws, he will need to have his pads toughened up or will need to wear dog boots (see Chapter 3 for more about toughening up paws and Chapter 4 for more about dog boots).

4. **Take along plenty of water.** An ample supply of water is imperative for comfort and safety. Your dog will drink a lot, especially on a hot day. If you take plastic bags for cleaning up behind your dog, bring an extra to use as a water bowl. Simply fold down the sides and fill the bag with a small amount of water. Don't let your dog drink too much or too fast. It is better to give him smaller amounts of water more often. Remember that drinking directly from a stream or lake could be dangerous for your dog (see Chapter 9 for more about water safety).

5. **Protect yourself and your dog from the elements.** You may need sunscreen, sunglasses, and a hat. Or you may need warmer clothes or rain gear. Think through your adventure and be prepared. Don't forget your dog's sweater.

6. **Bring along emergency supplies.** Even for a short hike, take a first-aid kit for you and your dog (see Chapter 10 for what to include in a first-aid kit). For longer hikes, also include matches, a sweater or jacket, a flashlight, map and compass, and some emergency food.

7. **Take lots of breaks and watch for fatigue.** Taking breaks helps you slow down and look around, see the sights, smell the smells, hear the sounds. Taking breaks will also help you avoid fatigue. If you or your dog are too tired, you are more likely to get hurt, disoriented, or lost. Have fun, but respect your limits. The signs of fatigue in a dog are slowing down, stopping often to rest, or losing enthusiasm in the activity. If you notice any of these signs, head back to camp. If your dog starts to limp, pants heavily, takes air in short, raspy breaths, stop immediately—your dog may be close to collapse. Give your dog a good long rest or carry him back to camp. *Stop before your dog reaches his limits.*

8. **Bring a snack.** Even on the shortest hikes, most people work up an appetite. Bringing along a little snack will remind you to take a rest break. Bring a couple of biscuits for your dog, too.

Paw Note: If you like to hike long distances but have a smaller dog that can't go as far, try a dog carrier. You can purchase one from a pet-supply store or fashion one from a canvas baby carrier by cutting a hole for the tail. Your small dog can walk as far as he can, then ride the rest of the way. (See Appendix H for dog carriers.)

Swimming

Camping near rivers, lakes, or the ocean can be terrific fun, especially in the hot summer months. A quick jump in the water can cool you and your dog. You can swim together or you can throw a toy or ball for your dog to retrieve.

Some dogs are always ready to swim.

If you have one of those dogs that loves to swim, you will probably be more concerned with managing when and where than with teaching how. Be careful around swift currents and waves. Even the strongest of swimmers can get into trouble in rough water.

Many dogs need to be taught to swim. Even if you have a reluctant dog, watch out once he learns to swim. You may discover a swimmer beneath that water-shy dog. Of course, some dogs really don't care for the water under any circumstance. In that case, don't force the issue. Teach him to swim enough so that he won't panic if he accidentally falls in the water, and leave it at that.

Teaching Your Dog to Swim

For a reluctant swimmer: Teach your dog to swim in a place where the water is calm and the temperature comfortable, such as in a pool or lake. Take him into the water far enough so that his feet won't touch the bottom. Support him under his chest and praise him when his feet start to move. Point him toward the shore and let go; as he swims, clap your hands and praise him. If you are teaching him in a pool, help him learn how to get out of the pool.

Use caution when teaching your dog to swim. Most dogs will immediately head for dry land when pointed in that direction, but some dogs will panic and try to climb on you. If that happens, calmly point your dog toward shore again and help him start in that direction.

Take your dog out swimming several times until he seems relatively comfortable in the water. Even if he never becomes a water enthusiast, he'll be much safer knowing how to swim.

For dogs that retrieve: Take your dog to a place where the water is calm with a gradually sloping shore. A pool, pond, lake, or quiet area of beach will work. It helps if the water isn't too cold. Bring a favorite retrieve toy—one that will float. Start by tossing the toy into the water where the dog can easily retrieve it while keeping his feet on solid ground. Slowly toss the ball farther into the water, no more than six inches farther with each toss. Let your dog get used to splashing through the water after the toy without swimming. He'll start to feel more secure moving in the water.

> ***Paw Note:*** *Caution! Water play, while terrific fun, also presents its own set of hazards. Keep your eye on your dog the entire time he is swimming. Never let a dog swim in a slip, choke, or training collar of any kind. These types of collars can get caught on underwater obstacles such as branches and can pull your dog under. Snapping turtles, water snakes, currents, and cold water can also place your dog at risk. Please read carefully the section in this book on water hazards (Chapter 9), and use caution and good sense when letting your dog swim.*

Take your time with this. The idea is to build up your dog's confidence around water without any surprises. When your dog is comfortably splashing in and out of the water after the toy, start tossing it a little farther out (again, no more than six inches or so at a time). When you toss it just beyond where your dog can reach, he will take just a tiny swim after the toy. As he's swimming for the toy, give him lots of praise. Have him do two or three small swims after the toy, then stop for the day.

Repeat this a few times in several days or weeks, starting slowly each time. Let him get used to the water again, but gradually increase the swimming distance. Soon your dog will be happily swimming after his toy on a regular basis.

Biking

Most dogs love to run alongside bikes. A combination of the joy of running, the chasing instinct, and the desire to keep up with their people propel dogs along on roads and trails. Whether you enjoy road biking or mountain biking, your dog can join you.

The most important aspects of biking with your dog are your control and your dog's temperament. A dog that has mastered the heel command, is well socialized, has an even temperament, and is in excellent shape is the easiest to train for biking along roads and wider trails. You can teach your dog to heel to the bike, and off you go on your adventure. Never try to hold onto your dog's leash while riding a bike if your dog is likely to try and chase every movement in the bushes or bark at other dogs. This is a setup for an accident. Back up and socialize your dog first, then train him to heel to the bike.

Another option is a bicycle-mounted leash device that allows your dog to run alongside you while you keep both hands on the handlebars. The most readily available of these contraptions is called The Springer. The manufacturer claims that this device absorbs 90 percent of the force of unexpected tugs on the leash, allowing you to keep your balance more easily.

If your dog is under voice control and you are in an area where dogs are allowed off leash, you can train your dog for mountain-bike adventures. You will have to decide whether to teach your dog to run behind the bike or in front (many trails are too narrow for your dog to travel alongside). If you teach your dog to run behind, you'll have much less chance of his running in front of your bike and causing an accident. However, you'll have to be checking over your shoulder frequently to make sure that he's keeping up and not getting too tired. Having your dog in front lets you keep your eyes on him easily but also means that he is leading the way and you are less in control. If he stops suddenly or crosses in front of you, you may crash.

Some mountain-bike enthusiasts have trained their dogs to run either ahead or behind while on a leash. This can work, but the leash itself can create a hazard if it gets tangled in the wheels.

You'll need to evaluate the type of biking you plan to do and train your dog accordingly. The training may take some time, but it's well worth the effort for the fun of biking with your dog.

 Paw Note: Use caution! Biking is one of the easiest ways to fatigue your dog. Condition your dog well before embarking on a bicycle adventure. Always travel at a slow, consistent pace. Your dog should be at a fast walk or an easy trot, not an all-out run. If you want to ride fast and hard, leave your dog at home. Look for signs of fatigue such as heavy panting, watch for your dog starting to lag behind, and check his paws often. Stop and rest frequently. Make sure that your dog has plenty of water, but don't let him drink too much at once or he can cramp up while running. If your dog shows signs of fatigue, stop immediately. Let him rest and then continue at a slower pace. If he is too tired, walk instead of riding.

Stick, Ball, and Frisbee

What do you do when you want to relax in camp, read a good book, or watch for birds, but your dog wants to play, play, play? Try a game of stick, ball, or Frisbee. Most dogs will wear out quickly playing this game. They will burn their energy and leave you plenty of time to read that good book.

Climbing and Other Agility Challenges

I have a dog that loves to climb trees. In order to temper her desire to climb too high, we practice agility games on lower branches. By turning her desire to climb into an agility exercise, she still gets to play in the tree and I have control over her safety.

Always have your dog practice climbing on low branches, such as those in oak trees. Use treats to control your dog's movements, having him slowly climb up and down. Be extra careful to teach your dog to climb down rather than jump. A dog that jumps from even a low branch can easily suffer a broken bone.

After a good game of Frisbee, you both can relax.
PHOTO COURTESY MARY KROSKE AND JEAN FAIRBANKS

*Your dog may find many agility challenges
while camping.*

Another agility challenge that you might encounter while camping is crossing a stream on a log. Some dogs are natural at this, but other dogs are timid and hesitant to cross. You can teach your dog to walk across a log by walking through the stream next to the log while guiding your dog across. If your dog is hesitant, you can use a treat to guide him across. Yes, your feet will get wet, so save this for a time when you can take off your shoes and let your feet dry out.

 Paw Note: *When you play agility games with your dog, have him wear a wide, flat, nylon or leather collar—never a choke chain, slip collar, or pinch collar. The collar must fit snugly to minimize the risk of twisting if it becomes caught on a branch.*

When you offer your dog an agility challenge, it is important to teach him control. Dogs will normally rush through activities with enthusiasm, but teaching your dog to move through or across obstacles slowly and with control will make him an overall safer hiker and camper. To learn about agility, try taking a class or reading an agility training book.

Find It!

Some dogs naturally love to track and find objects and people. Other dogs will need a little more encouragement to participate in this game.

If your dog loves to find and retrieve objects, you can start off with just about anything. Have your dog sit or lie down. Show him the item to be retrieved, then hide it nearby. Tell your dog to find it and let him search until he does. When your dog finds the item, lavish him with praise.

If your dog is new to the game, start off with a favorite toy and let him watch where you place it. Then lead your dog to the toy. When he goes to pick it up, say, "Find it," and then praise your dog. After a few times, your dog will start to go to the object on his own. When he can do this, start placing the object behind a tree or rock, just out of sight. Before you know it, your dog will be a "Find it" fanatic.

If your dog is really not interested or is confused, try this game using a dog biscuit as the object to be found. You may be surprised at how fast he catches on if you use food.

Hide and Seek

For another version of the "Find It" game, you can be the object to be found. I play this game at the beach with my dogs. I have them stay in place until I can hide behind some rocks, then I yell, "Jesse, Blue, come and find me!" They come tearing around the rocks, trying to figure out where I have gone. This is also a great game for reinforcing the come command.

Star Gazing

If you and your dog have tried all of the above activities, or even just a few, by the end of the day you will both be completely exhausted. But don't let your exhaustion deter you from star gazing. In fact, at the end of a hard day of traveling, camping, and hiking, you'll find nothing quite as rewarding as lying on your back and staring at the stars. Your dog will curl up beside you, you'll keep each other warm, and the night sky will come to life.

If you are new to star gazing, include in your camping gear a simple star chart. The sky changes throughout the evening, and what you see at 9 p.m. will be different than what you see at 1 a.m. Orient yourself by finding the Big Dipper, then move on, searching out the constellations. You and your dog may want to give special attention to finding Canis Major and Canis Minor. Look for Canis Major just southeast of Orion. Even if you can't find the constellations, you're sure to see a falling star or two.

You and your dog may enjoy looking for Canis Major
and Canis Minor while star gazing.

Sing Around the Campfire

I've known several people who have actually taught their dogs to sing. One friend's dog would carry a tune and bark out the song. Another friend taught her dog to bark at opportune moments during the song. For example, "She'll be coming around the mountain when she comes," "Woof! Woof!" Another great option is to make up new words to old tunes using your dog's antics as inspiration.

If your dog likes to sing, try a chorus of campfire songs.

Ghost Stories

This suggestion is mainly for the people, but it might surprise you to see how engrossed a dog can get during a good ghost story. Maybe it's the rhythm of the voice or the energy surrounding the campfire—or maybe the dog knows something you don't. Of course, if you happen to be roasting marshmallows at the same time, you may notice your dog's attention level taking another jump.

Be sure to include dog characters in your ghost stories. *Remember the one about the three-legged dog that lived behind the abandoned mine shack . . .*

These are our favorite camping activities. There are many more, such as skijoring, sledding, and tracking. But perhaps even more important than the specific activity is simply to remember to take time to see the world through your dog's eyes. Enjoy what he enjoys, notice what he notices. Live and camp at least part of the time through your dog's experience. Live like a dog: play when you're bored, rest when you're tired, eat when you're hungry, and explore every little sight, sound, and smell. Following these dog guidelines for life, you may even find a little of the dog spirit entering your soul. Watch out— before you know it, camping with your canine will seem like the most important activity in the world.

Many dogs enjoy a good ghost story.

CHAPTER EIGHT

GETTING ALONG WITH WILDERNESS CREATURES

One of the reasons why we camp is to experience Mother Nature's wonders, including our wild neighbors. It gives us a chance to associate with many other species, from ants to bears. While some people worry that camping with dogs actually scares off the wildlife, nothing can be further from the truth. Realistically, wild animals probably don't see dogs as any more of a threat than they see people as a threat. Dogs and humans alike are intruders. While both can create havoc for wildlife, dogs, like people, can also be respectful visitors. In fact, dogs can actually help us see and experience other animals.

Dogs have tremendous senses of hearing and smell. They know an animal is approaching before people can see it. If you pay attention to your dog's cues, you will be able to see wildlife that you otherwise would miss. Dogs can also pose a danger for wildlife. And certainly, wildlife can pose a danger for your dog. Melissa found this out when hiking with her two dogs, Jasper and Horton, near Homer Lake in Illinois.

Jasper and Horton were romping off leash through a heavily forested area. They were sticking close to Melissa, but because the trees were so dense, Melissa would momentarily lose sight of the two dogs. It was at one of these moments, when Jasper and Horton were out of sight, that the commotion started. First, Jasper started barking in a hysterical, high-pitched tone. Melissa called Jasper and Horton to her, and she could tell from the sounds in the dense growth that the dogs had started to return to her. But then Horton started barking, too. His hound dog bark, "Woo, woo, woo," also had taken on a hysterical quality. Melissa saw Horton backing out of the dense growth, still barking, and it was then that she heard the unmistakable crash that told her a large animal was close by in the trees. Suddenly Jasper came tearing through the trees and ran straight to Melissa, blood dripping from his side.

Melissa took hold of both dogs, quickly leashing Horton and gathering the fourteen-pound Jasper in her arms. Both dogs were frightened, so she struggled to settle them down, then hurried along the path away from the sound in the trees. Melissa was not sure of the extent of the wounds on Jasper as she walked the distance back to her car. She could not tell what had caused them. She did know that her shirt was getting covered in blood. She also knew that Jasper had become very quiet and stoic.

Melissa reached her car in record time and rushed Jasper to the nearest veterinary hospital. When the veterinarian shaved Jasper, they all gasped when they saw the wounds—a perfect row of teeth marks running down both sides of Jasper's body. They could only suppose that such wounds were created when she was picked up and shaken by a larger animal. Could it have been a wild dog? A bear? A cougar? They had no way of knowing for sure.

Jasper recovered from her wounds completely. Horton the hound dog got over the trauma. And Melissa now has a great story to tell—one that teaches everyone how dangerous the wilderness can be to your dog.

There are as many different types of wild animals as there are places to travel. Many will blend into the whole camping experience. They are of little consequence to your dog either way—neither creating a danger for your dog, nor your dog creating a danger for them. Others, from the smallest flea to the largest grizzly bear, can pose a real threat to your dog. And your dog can pose an equal or greater threat to their well-being. When you are camping with your dog, it is essential that you keep him safe from wildlife and wildlife safe from your dog.

Ticks, Insects, and Other Things That Crawl

What would camping be without a few ants, perhaps a mosquito or two buzzing around at dusk, and the honeybee that visits as you prepare your pancakes? For the most part, creatures that crawl and fly offer very little in the way of immediate, serious danger. You brush away the ants, cover yourself to avoid mosquito bites, and wait patiently for the bee to vacate the honey jar. Occasionally, however, the littlest of creatures can cause the biggest problems.

Fleas are creatures that most people with dogs know about—and know how to deal with. Fleas, for example, live around your home, and most people have to participate in active flea-control programs. Hopefully, when you embark on your camping trip, your dog will be flea-free and you will be winning your at-home battles.

While you are camping, you will still have to worry about these little, persistent creatures. Rodents and other animals carry fleas, and some of those fleas may carry diseases that pose a real danger to your dog. In the foothills near our house, for example, the flea population is actively spreading bubonic plague among the resident rodents. It is important that you keep up your flea-control efforts while you are camping. Running a flea comb through your dog's coat in the evening can help you look for those pesky fleas and remind you to check over your dog for any other hidden pests or injuries. You may also want to use a flea repellent while camping. Talk with your veterinarian about which products will work best for your dog. In addition, keep your dog away from rodent or squirrel holes.

Ticks are another common creature that you may encounter while camping. Ticks are found in most places in the United States and in many other countries, too. They live primarily in grassy and wooded areas and carry several diseases that can make your dog seriously ill.

Lyme disease is the most common illness associated with ticks and is now found in all areas of the United States. This is a serious illness that can cause joint pain, lameness, and fever. It affects the heart, the kidneys, and the nervous system. Rocky Mountain spotted fever and tick paralysis are two other diseases associated with ticks.

By checking your dog carefully and frequently while in tick country, you can help lower the risk of his catching a tick-related disease. You may also want to use a tick repellent such as an amitraz collar (Preventic is the brand, and the collar is available through veterinarians). This tick-specific collar keeps ticks from attaching to your dog long enough to spread disease. A pyrethrin dip or an over-the-counter tick and flea collar may also provide some protection. Ask your veterinarian about which tick control products would be best to use on your dog. In addition, consider having your dog vaccinated for Lyme disease.

These small creatures can cause big problems.
Check your dog carefully for ticks every day when camping.

Paw Note: To check your dog for ticks, run your fingers over every inch of his body, paying special attention to the areas between toes and around the ears where ticks can hide. To remove a tick that has attached itself to your dog, grasp it with tweezers as close to the base of the tick as possible. Twist counterclockwise while pulling gently until the tick comes out. If you don't have tweezers, you can use your fingernails, but tweezers work the best and are the safest. Be sure to get the whole tick and try not to leave the tick's head in your dog's skin. If the head is left in the dog, keep an eye on it in case it becomes infected. Also, watch the area around where the tick was imbedded. If redness or a rash develops, or if your dog seems lethargic or weak, is limping, or is otherwise ill, take him to a veterinarian. Also, check yourself for ticks. People are also susceptible to Lyme disease and other diseases spread by ticks.

Bees, wasps, yellow jackets, hornets, and **ants** are all insects that you may encounter on your camping trip. For the most part, a sting from one of these insects, while uncomfortable and even painful, will not cause a serious problem for your dog—unless your dog is allergic. (See Chapter 10 for more about signs of allergic reactions and how to administer first aid.) Still, you'd be wise not to let your dog chase or snap at bees and other stinging creatures or he may end up with a sting in his mouth or nose. Multiple stings from bees or ants are another problem altogether and can be serious. Keep your dog away from nests, and be careful not to pitch your tent on an ant mound.

Paw Note: If your dog gets stung by a bee, wasp, or hornet, you will need to make sure that the stinger is out. Check the area of the sting carefully. If the stinger is still in the dog, grasp it at the base closest to the dog's skin and pull it straight out. Be careful not to squeeze the sack on the end of the stinger. This holds the venom, and you may accidentally squeeze more into your dog.

Mosquitoes seem somewhat benign, but they carry the deadly heartworm parasite that can cause serious illness and death in dogs. While heartworms can be treated, the treatment is sometimes as dangerous as the parasite. Your best bet is to have your dog on preventative medication. Heartworms are found now in most parts of the United States. If your dog is not already on heartworm medication, check with your veterinarian about getting him started before you head out on your camping excursion.

Spiders and Scorpions

You will find only two types of **spiders** in the United States that pose any real threat to your dog. The **black widow** is about one inch long including legs and has an hourglass-shaped red mark on its belly. Black widows are found all over the United States. They hang out in dark places and will usually only bite if their nest is disturbed. A bite from a black widow spider can be serious for a dog. Generally, the initial bite is fairly painless, but within an hour, your dog will have stomach and back pains and possibly a fever and vomiting. You will need to get your dog to a veterinarian as soon as possible if he is bitten by a black widow.

The **brown recluse spider** has a small body and long legs; its total size, including legs, is about one and one-half to two inches long. It has a dark mark on its back that is violin-shaped. The spider is found mainly in the South. While the bite from a brown recluse is fairly painless, a blister will develop on the skin within a few hours. You will not need to give any specific first aid for a brown recluse spider bite, but get your dog checked by a veterinarian fairly soon afterward. The blister will turn into an ulcer and may affect the surrounding skin. The ulcer will need to be surgically removed so that it doesn't cause additional damage.

While most **scorpions** are not dangerous, two species that live in the Arizona, New Mexico, and California desert areas are poisonous. Their stings can cause extreme pain, difficulty in breathing, and paralysis. If your dog is stung by a poisonous scorpion, he should be seen by a veterinarian as soon as possible.

To avoid spider bites and scorpion stings, always keep your tent screen zipped up tightly and shake out sleeping bags, clothing, and shoes that have been left outside. Don't let your dog sniff around piles of wood or dark areas.

Snakes, Lizards, and Toads

With a few notable exceptions, your dog will pose more of a risk to snakes, lizards, toads, and frogs than they will to him. With all of the nonpoisonous varieties of reptiles and amphibians around, one is likely to slither across your path or through your campsite. Make sure that your dog leaves it alone and the creature will likely continue on its way without incident. Even the poisonous varieties are typically shy and elusive. But they can also be deadly.

Snakes may cause the biggest worry, and snakebites are more common than you might imagine. There are four types of snakes in the United States that can cause a dog serious harm—rattlesnakes, copperheads, cottonmouths, and coral snakes. One or more of these four snakes are found in almost every state in the continental United States. You should check in with a ranger or campground personnel to find out what kinds of snakes live in the area you will be visiting and how best to avoid them.

Rattlesnakes are one of the four poisonous varieties of snakes that may cross your path.

If you are in an area with a heavy snake population, keep your dog with you at all times and have your dog wear a bell on his collar to scare off snakes. Snakes are essentially shy creatures and will usually avoid a confrontation. If they know that you and your dog are coming, they will get out of the way.

If you are backpacking or camping in an area with poisonous snakes and will not have access to a veterinary hospital, talk with your veterinarian about adding snakebite medication to your first-aid kit. You may also want to consider carrying a snakebite kit. When I've hiked in Southern California and other desert areas, I've always carried one. They are tricky to use, and most experts agree that if you don't really know how to use the kit, you may do more harm than good in an emergency. If you do carry a snakebite kit, learn to use it before you head out on your trip. See Chapter 10 for first-aid treatment of snakebite.

Only two types of **lizards** pose any real danger to dogs—the Gila monster and the Mexican beaded lizard. Both are found in the southwestern United States and are so shy that the chance of your dog being bitten by one is small. Still, if you are traveling into their territory, use caution and keep your dog with you.

Several types of **toads** produce a venom from their glands that can poison a dog if the dog licks or mouths them. Two types of Bufo toads can kill a dog with their poison within a few minutes of exposure. One is the Colorado Toad; it is found near streams and wet areas of the southwestern desert. The other is called the Marine Toad; it lives throughout Florida and the South. With other toads, the risk depends on the type of toad and how much of the venom gets into the dog's mouth. Your best bet is to know if there are poisonous toads in the area that you are visiting, then keep your dog away from them.

Birds and Rodents

Dogs harass birds by chasing them and disrupting their nests, especially birds that nest in bushes or on the ground, and I've been told many stories about dogs catching rats and other rodents. But there are two areas of caution with birds and rodents. A large bird of prey, such as a hawk, an eagle, or an owl can easily carry off a small dog. I heard a story about a small white dog that escaped from his leash one evening and ran through a field of grass. Before the dog's people could catch up with him, he was swooped up by an owl and never seen again. A small dog running through a field doesn't look a lot different than a rabbit.

With rodents, the main concern is disease. You already heard about fleas and the diseases that can be passed from rodents to dogs via these pesky creatures. In addition, a bite from a rodent can transmit disease, including rabies. One important note about rabies: Even if your dog has been vaccinated, he may still be susceptible. The vaccination is not 100 percent effective.

Also, as a dog owner and conscientious camper, you have the responsibility not to feed birds, squirrels, and other cute wildlife that may visit your camp. Not only will the animals become used to people food and forgo their more nutritious natural diet, but an animal that is fed people food while dogs are around may start to view dogs as their friends. Even if your dog would never hurt a squirrel or sparrow, the next dog to visit the camp might. If squirrels or birds become accustomed to people with dogs feeding them, they may not be as cautious as they should be with other dogs.

Porcupines, Skunks, and Raccoons

Porcupines are fun little animals to watch. They move slowly and carefully down a path, waddling as they go. But porcupines are a real danger to dogs. Their quills have barbed ends, and once they pierce your dog's mouth or nose, they are tough to get out. Unlike the cartoon images, porcupines do not "throw" their quills. If your dog gets a face full of quills, you'll know that he was close enough to bite the animal. Keeping your dog away from porcupines is the best way to avoid having to take your dog to the veterinarian to have the quills removed.

Another shy but common creature that can quickly put a damper on a camping trip is the **skunk**. Skunks are essentially pacifists, partly because they have such an effective defense mechanism against dogs and other animals that choose to harass them—that pungent spray. A skunk's spray is something like mace or pepper spray and will sting a dog's eyes and skin as well as causing an unpleasant odor. Once your dog has been sprayed, you will have to deal with that awful smell.

Even the friendliest of dogs can get into trouble on the trail.

Paw Note: If your dog gets sprayed by a skunk, you'll first want to wash out his eyes, if possible with artificial tears or isotonic saline. Then get ready to bathe him. You will have to wash your dog in one of the commercial shampoos formulated to remove skunk odor or else in the old-fashioned way in tomato juice. Wet your dog down first, then lather him up with tomato juice. Rinse and repeat until the odor begins to subside. A third remedy is to wash your dog with diluted Dawn dish soap, rinse well, then soak the dog in white vinegar. Repeat until the odor subsides. The dish soap cuts the oils and the vinegar neutralizes the smell much the way tomato juice does.

Raccoons are another concern for dogs. These animals are aggressive, invasive, incredibly cute, and hard to scare off. They also seldom lose if they fight with a dog. Their sharp claws and teeth give them a distinct advantage over even a dog that outweighs them. Keep raccoons away from your camp by keeping it cleaned up and by hanging your food or locking it in the trunk of your car. If raccoons do visit your camp in the middle of the night, you can try scaring them off by making a lot of noise, but don't let your dog do the job for you. He is sure to come out the loser in a scuffle with a raccoon.

Deer, Elk, and Moose

These animals seldom are dangerous to dogs, although in mating season, they can certainly become aggressive and their hooves and sharp horns can do some serious damage. Once, our dog friend Mattie took off after a deer, yelping excitedly as she chased the deer up a mountain. She thought she was having the time of her life until the deer turned and started chasing her. Mattie was lucky and escaped, but the deer could have hurt her badly.

Usually a dog chasing a deer through the forest is a much bigger worry for the deer than for the dog. Dogs, especially two or more together in a pack, can literally run a deer into the ground. Even if the dogs tire of the chase, they can separate the deer from her family or tire her so that she becomes a target for other predators.

Wild Dogs, Mountain Lions, and Bears

Coyotes and wolves tend to be shy and avoid confrontation with domestic dogs. But it does happen. Wild dogs can carry diseases to your dog, and in a fight, your dog is sure to lose. If you are traveling in areas with wolves or coyotes, keep your dog near you.

Mountain lions or cougars are not very common, but in recent years, their numbers have increased in some western states, and many park areas are posted with mountain lion warnings. If you are traveling in an area with mountain lions, keep your dog on leash at all times. Dogs are just about the right size for a mountain lion's dinner. You will also want to keep children nearby and should never hike alone in mountain lion country.

If you see a mountain lion, do not run. Instead, make yourself as big as you can, standing tall and raising your arms over your head. Speak in a loud but calm voice. If you can, throw things at the mountain lion to scare him off, but never bend over to pick up a rock or stick. Keep your dog on leash and close to you.

When I first started camping about twenty years ago, I spent some time in Yellowstone and Yosemite national parks. On both trips, I hoped—prayed, really—that I would catch sight of a **bear**. Now that I know better, I am glad that my prayers were never answered. The black bear is the one you are most likely to encounter on a camping trip. Truthfully, most black bears keep to themselves. But with the rising bear population and the fact that more and more of their territory is being eaten up by housing developments, black bears are becoming a more common sight both in and out of the wilderness. As a result, they are more often tempted by the easy access to people food.

In addition, bears are smart. Bears scare hikers into dropping their packs, can get into all but the most ingenious and foolproof food containers, and recognize fast-food wrappers and ice chests. If you are camping in an area with bears, particularly bears that have been spotted near people, it will probably be posted as bear territory and give guidelines for storing your food. And as much as you may think you want to see a bear, your best bet, especially when traveling with your dog, is to avoid bears at all costs.

Here are some ways to minimize your chances of a bear encounter:

- Don't visit areas that are known for their recent bear encounters. Pick a different camp area instead.
- On the trail, make noise by talking or singing and have your dog wear bells. You don't want to surprise a bear.
- Keep your dog on leash at all times in bear country—no exceptions.
- Don't bring along or wear any scented items like deodorant, suntan lotion, or lip balm because they attract bears. Use only unscented items. When you camp, store all scented items, including toothpaste and medications, with your food.
- Cook all of your food 100 yards downwind from your tent. Never store food or even clothes in which you've cooked inside your tent.
- Follow all food-storage recommendations. Either use a metal bear box or a bear-proof canister, or hang your food.
- If you must store food in your car, put it in the trunk or cover it with a blanket, because bears can recognize ice chests, fast-food containers, and more. They will break a car window to get to food.

How to Hang Your Food
1. Take your food and divide it into two stuff sacks with about equal weight in each.
2. Tie one end of a rope to one of the stuff stacks and the other end to a rock or stick—something that will be easy to throw over a branch or guy wire.

3. Many camp areas, even wilderness areas, have strung up guy wires for hanging food out of a bear's reach. If they are available, use these wires. If not, you will need to find a suitable branch. Look for one that is about twenty feet in the air or higher and that hangs out away from the tree. Make sure that it is not so thick to allow a bear to climb out on it.
4. Throw the rock end of the rope over the branch or wire. Pull your stuff sack up as high as possible.
5. Now, as high as you can reach, tie the other stuff sack to the rope. Take the extra rope and put it into the stuff sack.
6. Take a long stick and push the stuff sack up until the two bags hang at the same height. The bags should be at least twelve feet off the ground.
7. In the morning, you'll pull one side down with the long stick, then lower the other sack.
8. If you are camping in an area without trees, you can hang your food off a cliff or high rock—anything with a steep face that a bear cannot climb.

Paw Note: If you are traveling in an area with grizzly bears or their close cousins, the brown bears, leave your dog at home. Grizzlies can weigh up to 1,400 pounds and are easily riled by dogs. In the United States, you are likely to encounter grizzlies in only Glacier and Yellowstone national parks and in parts of Alaska.

Domestic Animals

Dogs are more of a risk to domestic animals like sheep or cattle than they are to dogs. In many parts of the country, however, it is legal to shoot dogs that are harassing domestic animals. I know one dog that was shot for chasing a sheep—he now has only three legs. He was lucky to come away with his life. Keep your dog under control around domestic animals, for their safety and for your dog's safety.

Visits from wildlife are one of the reasons why it is better to have your dog in your tent at night rather than leaving him tied up outside.

Find Out About the Wildlife

These are just some of the most common animals you may encounter while camping. Each area has its own animal population and ecology. Badgers, alligators, and jellyfish are a few examples of other animals that you may run into on a camping trip. Before you head out on a camping adventure, check with the ranger or campground officials and ask what types of wildlife you can expect to encounter and what precautions you will need to take. It is also a good idea to read up on the plants and animals of the region.

CHAPTER NINE

DOGGIE DANGERS

Water Hazards

When I think about dogs and water, I think about Blue merrily splashing through the waves at our favorite beach, chasing down the tennis ball, shaking off the salt and spray. But water, oceans, rivers, streams, lakes, and ponds all have very real hazards for dogs.

Giardia is a common water hazard, and almost all experienced campers and hikers have heard about or experienced the severe cramping and diarrhea associated with this organism. **Cryptosporidium** is another water parasite that produces similar symptoms. The Centers for Disease Control estimate that these two organisms now occur in 95 percent of untreated water sources in the United States. People often believe that dogs won't be affected by giardia and other water hazards. This is simply not true. The dehydrating diarrhea and cramping can make a dog as sick and miserable as it can make you.

So what can you do about giardia and other water pollu-
tants? First, keep your dog from drinking directly from natural
water sources. Give him plenty of filtered or treated water to
drink so that he is less likely to lap from the stream. If you are
in a campground that has drinking water, or if you brought
enough water from home, you'll be set. But if you are depending
on natural water sources such as rivers or streams, you will
have to purify the water. You have these options:

- You can use a water-filter system with a filter small enough
  to snag giardia and crypto organisms. It also gives you
  crisp, clear, delicious drinking water. Water filters by themselves don't necessarily get out all of the viruses that can
  inhabit water, but many of them are available with an additional iodine treatment. The only drawbacks to filters are
  that they are expensive (anywhere from $30 to $300) and
  heavy to carry backpacking. Many backpackers wouldn't
  use any other method, however.
- You can use iodine purification tablets. These are cheap and
  easy to carry, and they work for most viruses and organisms
  most of the time. They don't work for crypto, however. They
  also make the water taste like a swimming pool.
- You can boil your water for five minutes. This is a surefire
  way to kill all of the bad guys and make the water safe to
  drink, but it won't filter out the dirt and debris. It also takes
  time and stove fuel.
- You can also use a combination of the above techniques. Boil
  your cooking water, then filter and use iodine for straight
  drinking water.

Realistically, you can take every possible precaution and
still come down with giardia or crypto. Therefore, you should
always be prepared by carrying an antidiarrheal medication.
(See Chapter 10 for treatment of diarrhea.) Generally, symptoms from giardia don't appear for a few weeks, so unless you
are on an extended trip, you are more likely to have to deal
with it at home than while you are camping.

*Cold water and heavy currents are obvious hazards for your dog.
Water may have other hidden dangers, such as
giardia and cryptosporidium.*
PHOTO COURTESY PENNY AND MIKE BROZDA

Leptospirosis is a common water disease found in areas with grazing animals. Dogs are generally protected from leptospirosis through their regular vaccinations (the "L" in your dog's DHLP vaccination is for leptospirosis). This vaccine is given routinely once a year, but some veterinarians recommend giving it to a dog every six months when traveling in wilderness areas.

Another serious water hazard is **algae bloom**. Although algae-bloom poisoning is rare, when all of the conditions are right this is a real hazard for your dog. The symptoms are severe and deadly. Dogs that drink or eat a concentration of algae bloom usually start vomiting within an hour or two and are often dead a few hours later. There is no antidote for this poisoning.

Algae usually grows in standing or slow-moving water.
You'll often see it in ponds or stagnant pools, and it gives the
water a green or gray tinge. If you are around water that has
algae, *keep your dog out of it.*

Water currents can also be dangerous for your dog. Moving water, rapids, and waves can be a risk even for good swimmers. Sometimes underwater branches, plants, and debris can
snag a dog. Use good judgment when you let your dog swim.
Keep him out of moving currents and waves that are beyond his
abilities. Always supervise your dog when he is swimming and
make your dog come out of the water before he becomes too
tired. A tired dog is definitely at a higher risk of drowning.

Cold water is another hazard for dogs. Swimming in cold
water can cause cramps, making your dog unable to swim back
to shore. Getting chilled and then being in the cold air and wind
can also put your dog at risk for hypothermia.

Hypothermia

Cold weather, water, and windchill all play a part in a dog's
chance of getting **hypothermia**. Hypothermia occurs when the
body temperature drops below normal. Individual dogs, depending on their coat, their level of fitness, and the environmental
conditions, will be affected differently by the cold. For example,
a dog that has been swimming in a snowmelt stream can
become very chilled from the wind, even if the air temperature
doesn't seem that cold to you. Short-haired dogs such as Dalmatians and Whippets are much more susceptible to cold conditions. Pay attention to your dog's temperature and don't wait
until he starts shivering to warm him up.

Wet weather is not the only condition surrounding
hypothermia. **Traveling in the snow** can also put your dog at
risk. While you are wearing boots, snow pants, gloves, and hats,
your dog may only have his fur coat for protection. You may
need to keep your dog warm with dog boots and a sweater, and
make sure that your dog does not get chilled in camp and at
night. Give him a place near the campfire and a warm bed.

*Most dogs love snow, but you will have to make sure
that they don't get too cold.*

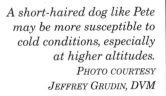

*A short-haired dog like Pete
may be more susceptible to
cold conditions, especially
at higher altitudes.*
PHOTO COURTESY
JEFFREY GRUDIN, DVM

Altitude can also affect your dog's ability to withstand cold. A dog that travels to higher altitudes, especially if he is not accustomed to it, can get tired more easily and have a harder time warming up his body. You will need to pay special attention to your dog's needs if you are traveling above 8,000 feet.

Exposure to cold temperatures can also cause **frostbite**. This is the freezing of small areas of the body. A dog's paws, nose, and ears are at particular risk when traveling in cold weather. Be diligent about checking your dog's paws for ice, snow, mud, and salt when you travel in cold weather.

For first-aid treatment of hypothermia and frostbite, see Chapter 10.

Heat and Heatstroke

Most summertime campers have to contend with the possibility of heat exposure. Hot weather, lots of sun, and dehydration can all be very real, serious risks for dogs. As with cold exposure, prevention is the best answer. Here are the ways heat will affect your dog:

• Walking over hot surfaces such as sand, pavement, or rock can cause sores and blistering on a dog's feet. If you are in the heat, check your path frequently with your hand. If it is hot to your touch, it may be too hot for your dog to walk on "bare pawed." Try lightweight boots to protect his feet.

• Dogs need more water when they are camping, hiking, and playing than they do when they are at home—sometimes two to three times as much water to keep them from getting dehydrated. Be sure to take lots of water breaks. It is better to give your dog smaller amounts of water more often than to let him guzzle down a bowl at the end of the day.

 Paw Note: *See page 158 for symptoms and treatment of dehydration.*

- **Sunburn** is a problem for light-haired dogs, especially those with very short hair or exposed pink skin. Protect your dog from sunburn by providing him with shade or covering. You may also want to use a sunscreen. Check with your veterinarian about which human sunscreens are safe for dogs, or use one made for dogs.
- **Heatstroke,** or hyperthermia, is when the body temperature rises above normal. Heatstroke is most commonly seen in dogs left in cars during hot weather, but it can also happen easily if you are hiking or traveling by boat in hot weather. To prevent heatstroke, keep your dog cooled off by giving him plenty of water to drink, providing shade and rest breaks, and cooling him off with dunks in a stream. In extreme temperatures, or if your dog is susceptible to overheating, cool your dog by taking a towel or terry-cloth dog sweater, wetting it, and placing it over him. For first-aid treatment of heatstroke, see Chapter 10.

Dogs need protection from the sun, too.

Burns

Most dogs are not as cautious around fire as you might imagine they would be. A dog can get his whiskers singed around a campfire or cook stove, trying to get a bite of that delicious-smelling camp meal. Sparks or popping embers from the campfire can also singe a dog's fur. And the next morning, beware of your dog treading through last night's fire pit. Hot coals may sit below the surface. Beaches can be a particular hazard because fires are left to burn themselves out and fire pits are often just holes in the sand. A dog taking an early-morning romp across the beach could end up with burned paws.

Always keep a close eye on your dog around fires and use good judgment in finding that happy medium between letting your dog settle down next to the warm fire and keeping him away from popping embers.

Getting Lost

Dogs that chase other animals face a high risk of getting lost in the wilderness. Even a dog on leash can sometimes get lost. Not long ago, a friend of ours had her dog, Mocha, with her on a mountain bike trail when a rabbit shot out of the bushes just ahead of them. The dog literally tore the leash from our friend's hand and took off. Mocha's person immediately started looking for her. Luckily, a few miles away, Mocha ran into a pair of hikers who saw her dragging her leash and snagged her. Our friend's frantic search fortunately led her to the hikers and Mocha. If those hikers hadn't been there or acted as quickly as they did, however, Mocha may have gotten seriously lost.

What can you do? First, keep your dog on leash (and hang on tightly if a rabbit darts in front of you) and use good judgment when you let your dog off leash. Second, make sure that your dog has good ID. Keep an ID tag or a collar with special ID for camping. Have a phone number on the ID where someone can be reached. For example, if you are hiking in Colorado, you won't be answering your phone in California. Have a friend's or relative's number, or your veterinarian's number, on the tags for emergency backup. Consider having your dog tattooed or having an ID chip inserted. (See Chapter 5 for more about ID, tattooing, and ID microchips.)

Plant Hazards

Plants are usually thought of as peaceable members of the natural community, giving us lots of air to breathe, providing us with protection from the sun and weather, and producing a splendor of color and blooms. Yet a few notable plants also create dangers for dogs.

The seemingly benign **foxtail** is one of those dangers. This arrow-shaped grass seems primarily like a nuisance. It gets caught in your dog's fur and between toes and has to be dug out at the end of the day. But if you have lived or camped in foxtail country (which can be just about any grassland or meadow), you know that these little barbs climb up a dog's nose, dive into the soft skin between toes, and embed themselves in the side of a dog and slowly work their way toward a vital organ. A foxtail was actually found in the uterus of one of our dogs when she was spayed. Not only will these pesky plants cause innumerable veterinary bills, but the infections they cause can threaten your dog's health. Along with foxtails, **burrs, seeds, and thorns** can also work their way into soft skin, noses, and ears.

Protect your dog from the consequences of these plant parts by checking your dog every night before bed. Comb for foxtails, thorns, burrs, and seeds, as well as for fleas and ticks. If your dog exhibits the telltale massive sneezing fit associated with a foxtail finding its way up a nostril, get him checked out by a veterinarian as soon as possible.

Poisonous plants are also a danger for your dog, especially if he is one of those types that must put everything in his mouth. **Wild mushrooms, elderberries,** and **acorns** are just a few of the plants that can poison dogs. In fact, there are so many that it would be difficult to list them all. Your best bet is to find out about the plants in the area in which you are traveling, then take precautions to keep your dog away from those that are poisonous.

If you are traveling in the desert, you will have to be especially mindful of **cactus thorns**. Dogs can get stuck by cactus thorns from walking on them, brushing against a plant, or heading nose first into the plant after a quick-moving lizard.

Some dogs learn quickly about cactus thorns and avoid them; others get pricked over and over again while never quite making the association between the plant and the pain.

Poison Oak, Ivy, and Sumac

Your dog has a very small chance of getting the itchy, painful rash associated with these three plants, but it does happen occasionally. A more realistic fear is that you will get the oils from these plants on you from your dog. If your dog has been romping through poison oak and you pet him, you could end up with a horrible rash.

There are more preventions and cures for poison oak, ivy, and sumac than there is room to print—everything from preventative lotions to vinegar dips. Because we cannot give you every prevention and remedy available, here is one seven-step method that seems to work:

Watch out! These three plants can put a damper on an otherwise fine trip.

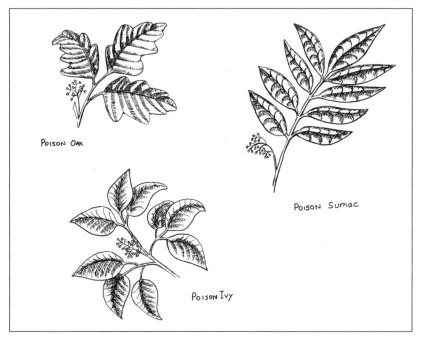

POISON OAK

POISON Sumac

POISON Ivy

1. Know if you are traveling in an area with poison oak, ivy, or sumac and learn to recognize the plant. Because these plants change seasonally, make sure that you can recognize it in spring, summer, fall, and winter.
2. Keep your dog out of it whenever possible. You may want to keep him on lead and discourage him from exploring off trail.
3. Wear protective clothing. Long sleeves and pants will help if you brush against the plant or if your dog brushes against you.
4. If you are highly reactive, use one of the commercial poison oak and ivy preventative lotions.
5. If you are exposed, do not touch your eyes or other sensitive areas. Wash yourself thoroughly as soon as possible (within thirty minutes is best) with cool water and a strong soap to cut the oil. Fels Naptha is a brand of bar laundry soap that works well for getting the oils off skin. Wash your clothes, too.
6. If your dog has been romping through poison oak, you'll need to wash him. Be sure to keep yourself covered and use gloves if possible when washing your dog. If you know you are susceptible to poison oak, ivy, or sumac, have someone else wash your dog.
7. It takes three to ten days for the rash to appear. If you are away from home in poison oak, ivy, or sumac country for more than three days, bring Calamine or Caladryl lotion along just in case.

Hunting Traps

If you are hiking in a hunting area, be cautious about hunting traps. Some are big enough to seriously injure a dog. Talk with the ranger or campground officials to get information about hunting in the area you are visiting.

Bloat

Bloat is not a camping-specific hazard, but because dogs often drink, eat, and exercise more when they camp, they may have an increased risk. Bloat is when a dog's stomach expands with gas. The stomach or intestine can then twist, causing a serious condition that is only treatable by a veterinarian.

While the exact cause of bloat is not really known, a couple of factors seem to contribute. Dogs with large, deep chests are more likely to suffer from bloat, and dogs that gulp their food or water seem to have a higher risk. Heavy exercise right before or after eating may also increase the risk. In addition, a dog that eats more than usual (he gets into the bag of dog food and eats the whole thing) may have a greater risk.

To avoid bloat, feed your dog two smaller meals a day instead of one big meal. Give your dog small amounts of water often, and discourage him from gulping down large quantities of food or water. Don't let your dog do strenuous exercise right before or after eating. If you see signs of bloat in your dog—distended stomach, dry vomiting, restlessness or discomfort when he tries to lie down—get your dog to a veterinarian right away. (For more about bloat, see Chapter 10.)

Dog boots help protect your dog's paws on hot, rough surfaces.
PHOTO COURTESY PEE DEE'S PAW PROTECTORS

CHAPTER TEN

BASIC FIRST AID

Important—Please Read This!

We, the authors of this book, readily admit that we are not veterinary medical professionals, nor are we qualified to give medical advice. The information presented in this chapter is drawn from sources believed to be reliable, and we have made every effort to ensure accuracy—including having the information reviewed by respected veterinarians. This section is intended to help you think through the kinds of emergencies that you may encounter while camping and to act quickly in an emergency situation. It is not meant to replace veterinary care, nor is it meant to be inclusive of all situations that may arise while camping. For more extensive information on first aid for dogs, see the books and resources listed in Appendix G and discuss emergency procedures with your veterinarian.

Your Basic First-Aid Kit

You will want to bring along a first-aid kit for you and your dog. You can buy a ready-made first-aid kit—special kits are made just for dogs—or you can modify a people first-aid kit to include items specific to dogs. You can also put together your supplies. It is probably easiest to put together a camping first-aid kit that suits your specific needs. When you return from a trip, you can replenish supplies that you may have used and put the kit away with your camping gear for the next trip. Just before you leave on a camping excursion, you can look through the kit and doublecheck the expiration dates on the medications. (See a suggested list of supplies on the next page.)

How to Approach an Emergency

Part of first aid is learning to think through an emergency situation and deciding what steps you should take.

What Should You Do if Your Dog Gets Hurt?

First, you need to assess the situation—figure out the extent of the injury. If your dog is limping, for example, you will have to see if he has a cut on his foot or a more serious injury, such as a broken bone. Sometimes the problem will be obvious or you will have seen the accident happen. Other times the cause and extent of the injuries may be more mysterious, or your dog may have multiple injuries.

Here are the steps to assess an injury:

1. Is your dog unconscious? If so, check for breathing and heartbeat (see pages 151-153 for steps on administering CPR).
2. If your dog is conscious, identify visible injuries. You may need to look over your dog's whole body. Check the following: (a) Is he bleeding? (b) Do you see any severe injuries, such as broken bones? (c) Is your dog alert and responsive?
3. Check your dog for symptoms of shock (see pages 154-155 for symptoms and first aid for shock).
4. Check for less obvious injuries. Look for tender or sore spots by running your hands over your dog's body. Be careful

FIRST-AID KIT FOR DOGS

Basic
- 2-inch roll gauze
- Nonstick gauze bandages
- Adhesive tape or vet wrap (this is also called sports wrap and sticks to itself instead of sticking to fur)
- Tweezers (the type on a Swiss Army knife work well)
- Small scissors for clipping fur (get good scissors—they are worth the extra expense)
- Antibiotic ointment (Neosporin, bacitracin, or calendula gel)
- Antiseptic wipes or soap (Betadine)
- Dog boots (if not already included with your gear)
- Hydrogen peroxide—3 percent solution (one tablespoon for every fifteen to twenty pounds of dog, to induce vomiting; repeat only once in ten minutes if no vomiting occurs; discuss appropriate use and proper dosage for your dog with your veterinarian)

Additional Items
- Cortisone cream
- Bag Balm
- Thermometer (ask your veterinarian to show you how to take your dog's temperature)
- Snakebite kit
- Instant cold pack
- Ace bandage
- Nail clippers
- Styptic powder (Kwik Stop)
- Saline eye wash

Medications (Talk with your veterinarian about using these medications in an emergency and the proper dosages for your dog):
- Antidiarrheal (Loperamide or Kaopectate)
- Antihistamine (Benadryl)
- Aspirin (use only if your veterinarian recommends aspirin for your dog. *Never* give your dog Tylenol or ibuprofen).

People Items
- Moleskin
- Regular bandages
- Anti-itch medication (Calamine or Caladryl)
- Lip balm

while doing this. If you hit a tender spot, your dog could react by trying to bite.

5. Decide which injuries or symptoms need immediate attention. Once you have made your assessment, you need to administer the proper care. The most critical procedures will first involve providing lifesaving techniques such as CPR or stopping bleeding. Treat shock next. Then continue with specific first-aid treatments, such as splinting or bandaging. If your dog has suffered a serious injury, consult with a veterinarian, even if your dog appears to have recovered.

What Do You Do if Your Dog Is Sick?

You will need to go through a similar set of assessment steps if your dog is sick. If your dog is vomiting, for example, you need to decide if the cause is dehydration, heat or cold exposure, a poisonous plant, a spider bite, or contaminated water. You also need to decide how serious the illness is to your dog. Start with these steps:

1. Is your dog unconscious? If so, check for breathing and heartbeat (see pages 151-153 for steps on administering CPR).
2. If your dog is conscious, identify all of the obvious symptoms: (a) Is your dog vomiting? Does he have diarrhea? (b) Does your dog appear disoriented? (c) Is your dog showing signs of being extremely tired or lethargic? (d) Does your dog appear to be too warm or too cold?
3. Try to identify the source of the illness. Is your dog suffering from heat or cold exposure? Could he have eaten or drunk anything poisonous? Does your dog have an injury that could have become infected? Does your dog have any other health problems that could be contributing to the illness?
4. If you are having trouble identifying the illness, check your dog carefully for signs of a spider bite or snakebite. Look for sore spots on his body or wounds on his legs, chest, or face.
5. Check your dog for symptoms of shock (see pages 154-155 for symptoms and first aid for shock).

6. If you have identified the reason for the illness, treat your dog for any life-threatening symptoms first, then proceed to specific first aid. If you have not identified the reason for the illness, treat the symptoms in order of severity and try to get your dog to a veterinarian as soon as possible. Always consult with a veterinarian if your dog has been seriously ill, even if he appears to recover fully.

How Do You Muzzle an Injured Dog?

Sometimes a dog that is hurt or scared will bite the person who is trying to help him, even if he would never bite under normal circumstances. You may need to muzzle your dog to protect yourself and to successfully administer first aid or move your dog to a veterinary hospital. Here are two ways to muzzle a dog in an emergency (see next page for illustration):

1. Take a piece of thin cloth or gauze bandage two to three feet long (do not use rope or twine). Make a loop and slip it quickly over the bridge of the dog's nose and mouth. Tighten down the loop firmly so that the dog cannot open his mouth. Then cross the cloth under the dog's chin and bring the ends behind the dog's ears. Tie behind the ears to keep the muzzle in place.
2. If you don't have a longer piece of material, you can take a short piece of cloth—a bandanna will work—and quickly wrap it around the bridge of the dog's nose and mouth, tying at the top. The key is to be quick so that your dog doesn't wiggle out of the muzzle before you get it tied on.

 Paw Note: Caution: *Never muzzle a dog that is having trouble breathing, because it can further constrict air flow. Never muzzle a dog that is vomiting, because it will increase the risk of choking. Never muzzle a flat-faced dog such as a Pug or Bulldog—these types of dogs may not be able to breathe properly when muzzled.*

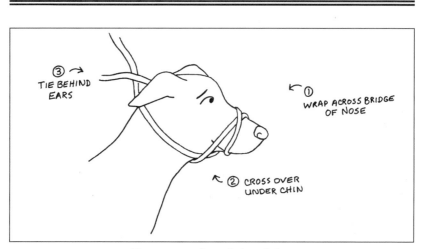

How to muzzle an injured dog.

How Can You Move an Injured or Sick Dog?

If your dog is hurt or sick, you may need to move him to get him to a veterinarian for treatment. If you have a smaller dog, you will probably be able to carry him. If you have a larger dog, these two techniques may help:

- Carry your dog across your chest with one arm between the front legs and one arm between the rear legs. This helps distribute the dog's weight, allowing you to carry him more easily.
- Make a litter by using poles or long sticks and a tarp, blanket, or sleeping bag. Place the sticks parallel to each other and wrap the blanket around them three times. Your dog's weight can keep the blankets from unwrapping.

What If My Dog Is Unconscious?

If your dog is unconscious, you will need to check his breathing and pulse. If he is not breathing or does not have a pulse, start administering CPR (see pages 151-153). If your dog is breathing, get him to a veterinarian as soon as possible. Try to keep your dog lying belly down while you transport him to the veterinarian; he will have an easier time breathing in that position.

Lifesaving Techniques for Camping Emergencies

CPR

You will need to administer CPR if your dog is not breathing or does not have a pulse. Check your dog's breathing by putting your face near his nose to feel his breath. You can also watch his chest to see if it is moving. If your dog *is* breathing, do *not* administer CPR.

If your dog is *not* breathing, start the ABCs (airway, breathing, circulation) of CPR:

A) **Check the dog's throat to see if an object or the dog's tongue is blocking the airway.** If something is blocking the airway, remove it if you can do so without being bitten. Use a pair of pliers if available. If you cannot easily remove the object, perform a modified Heimlich maneuver. For a large dog: Stand the dog on all fours, reach under his chest to the base of the rib cage, make a fist, and press up sharply three or four times. If the dog is unconscious, turn him onto his back and press hard at the base of the rib cage three or four times. For a small dog: Lift the dog by his hind legs, hang him upside down, and give three or four sharp compressions on his chest. Your dog may start breathing on his own once the airway is cleared.

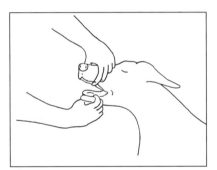

The first step in CPR is to check your dog's throat to make sure that the airway is not blocked by an object or the tongue.

B) **Once the airway is cleared, but your dog is still not breathing:** Cup your hands over the dog's mouth and nose and make a seal between your dog's nose and your mouth.

Once the airway is clear, if your dog is still not breathing, start mouth-to-nose resuscitation.

Breathe directly into your dog's nostrils. Breathe about one breath every three seconds. Breathe hard enough to see your dog's chest rise and fall.

C) If, after five breaths, your dog does not start breathing on his own: Check your dog for a heartbeat. Find your dog's shoulder blades with the palm of your hand. Bring your other hand opposite the shoulder blades on the chest. This is approximately where you will find the

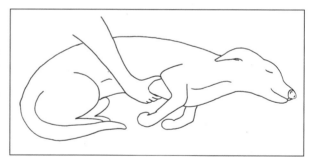

To find your dog's heartbeat, put your hand on his chest opposite the shoulder blades.

heartbeat. If you do not feel it, move your hand up and down on the chest to make sure that you cannot feel it in a different place. *If your dog has a heartbeat or pulse, even a faint one, do not do chest compressions. Continue assisted breathing.* Check every minute or so to see if your dog has started breathing on his own.

If your dog does not have a heartbeat: Place your dog on his right side. For a large dog, put one hand on top of the other (like you would when administering CPR to a person) on the dog's chest, just below the shoulders. For a small dog, put one hand on top of the dog's chest just below the shoulders and one hand under the chest. Press down on the chest in short, sharp compressions. Try to do about 100 chest compressions per minute for a larger dog and about 120 per minute for a smaller dog. Press down about one-third of the dog's chest width.

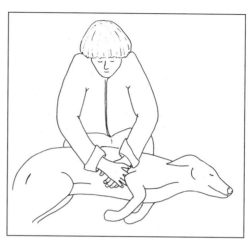

If your dog does not have a heartbeat, start chest compressions.

For smaller dogs, this is about one-half to one inch. For larger dogs, this is about one to two inches.

If you are doing CPR by yourself: Alternate breathing and chest compressions. Give one breath followed by five chest compressions.

If you are doing CPR with a partner: One person can breathe while the other person gives chest compressions. Give one breath every five chest compressions. Try to do the chest compressions at the rate of about 100 per minute for a larger dog and 120 per minute for a smaller dog. Check your dog's heartbeat every two minutes until his heart starts beating. If his heart starts beating but he is still not breathing, discontinue compressions and continue assisted breathing until he starts breathing on his own.

Continue CPR until the dog has a strong heartbeat and pulse, until you reach a veterinary hospital, or until twenty minutes have passed and your efforts have not been successful.

> **Paw Note:** *Sometimes it is hard to find a dog's heartbeat. You may want to feel around on your dog's chest now, before an emergency occurs, and figure out where to find it. If you are unclear about how to administer CPR, ask your veterinarian to show you before you go on a camping trip.*

Stopping Bleeding

To stop bleeding, put pressure directly on the wound with a clean cloth or gauze pad. If the bleeding stops easily, clean the wound and bandage it using an antibiotic ointment. If the bleeding does not stop easily, keep putting pressure on the wound for five to ten minutes. If the cloth or gauze pad becomes soaked, add a second cloth on top of it. Do not move the first cloth because that may disrupt the clotting of the blood. Continue adding layers of pressure bandages until the bleeding is controlled. If your dog has a wound that does not stop bleeding, keep pressure on it and get your dog to a veterinarian as soon as possible. You can maintain pressure on the wound while getting to the veterinarian by wrapping it with a bandage or tape.

Dealing with Shock

Shock is a critical state that occurs in a body that is shutting down. Your dog can go into shock if he is too hot or too cold, if he has been poisoned, if he is seriously ill, or if he has suffered a traumatic injury. If your dog goes into shock, you need to administer first aid immediately and get your dog to a veterinarian.

The early signs of shock include:

- Fast breathing or heavy panting
- Faster-than-usual heart rate (a normal heart rate in a large dog is about 60 to 100 beats per minute; in a small dog, about 100 to 160 beats per minute)
- Pale or bright red gums
- Weakness
- Restlessness or anxiousness

Signs of severe shock include:

- Shallow breathing
- Irregular or weak pulse
- Very pale or blue gums
- Dilated pupils
- Unresponsiveness or unconsciousness
- Coldness

To administer first aid for shock:

1. Deal with the immediate trauma, such as stopping bleeding or administering CPR as needed.
2. Wrap your dog in a blanket, towel, or even your jacket to keep him warm. This is very important. Your dog's body temperature can drop very quickly when he is in shock. If your dog is suffering from heatstroke, take steps to cool his body instead (see pages 160-161 for more about heatstroke).
3. If possible, do not let your dog move around. Keep him quiet and comfortable.
4. Do not let your dog drink.
5. If your dog has signs of shock, get him to a veterinarian as soon as possible.
6. If your dog becomes unconscious, check for breathing and pulse (see pages 151-153 for CPR).

Paw Note: A dog's normal gum color is pale pink to pale red. When pushed with your finger, it should get paler for a moment but return to normal color quickly. If your dog is in shock, the gums will be slow to return to normal color after being pressed. You may want to check your dog's gums under normal conditions to see his usual color.

First Aid for Specific Injuries and Illnesses

Allergic Reactions

Although it is uncommon, dogs can have allergic reactions to bee stings, mosquito and other insect bites, and to some medications. If your dog has an allergic reaction, he may experience hives, redness, swelling, difficulty in breathing, vomiting or diarrhea, and signs of shock.

To treat mild allergic reactions:

1. Wrap ice in a cloth or towel and place it on the bite to help reduce swelling.
2. Check for signs of shock (see pages 154-155 for signs of shock and first aid).
3. Consult with your veterinarian about further treatment to reduce itching and swelling.
4. If you cannot get to a veterinarian, you may want to give your dog an antihistamine such as Benadryl. Check with your veterinarian before you go camping to find out the right dosage and appropriate circumstances for giving your dog an antihistamine.

For a more severe allergic reaction:

1. Make sure that your dog's airway stays open. If your dog stops breathing, administer CPR (see pages 151-153).
2. Administer first aid for shock (see pages 154-155).
3. Get your dog to a veterinarian immediately.

Bloat

Bloat is a serious condition and should be treated by a veterinarian immediately. Early signs of bloat include mild agitation, minor abdominal pain, discomfort when lying down, or refusing to lie down. Later signs of bloat include when your dog tries to vomit but nothing comes out, when he tries to defecate but nothing comes out, drooling, distended stomach, and abdominal pain.

To check for bloat, palpate your dog's stomach by pushing gently. A normal stomach is soft and malleable. With bloat, the stomach becomes very hard and will sound like a drum if you thump on it.

Immediate veterinary treatment is essential.

Broken Bones

Broken bones are sometimes obvious. Other times, it may be hard to tell if a bone is broken or if the dog has another injury, such as a torn or strained muscle. Either way, proceed as if the bone is broken until it can be checked by a veterinarian.

For an injured leg:

1. If your dog can walk on three legs comfortably *and* the bone is stable, do not splint.
2. If the bone is unstable, meaning it is moving at the fracture site or is protruding through the skin, you need to consider splinting the leg.
3. Only splint broken bones below the elbow and below the knee. Never attempt to splint a broken bone above the elbow or knee.
4. Splint the leg by wrapping it with a towel or magazine. Tape or tie the splint on so that the leg is immobilized.
5. You can also make a splint by using two sticks or small, smooth branches. Tie or tape them to the leg.
6. Administer first aid for shock (see pages 154-155).
7. Get to a veterinarian as soon as possible.

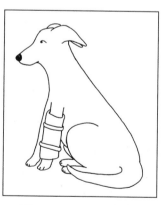

You can use a towel or magazine to splint an injured leg.

For an injury to the back, neck, shoulders, or ribs:

1. Immobilize the dog as much as possible. If you can, transport your dog on an inflexible object, such as a flat board.

2. If your dog can walk and resists being carried, then walking may be the safest. Go slowly!
3. If you must carry your dog, carry him against your chest with one arm between his front legs and the other arm between his rear legs. Try to keep his back straight.
4. Administer first aid for shock (see pages 154-155).
5. Get your dog to a veterinarian immediately.

Burns

Burns can be minor or severe, depending on how deep they are and how much of the body is burned.

For a small, mild burn:

1. Cool the area off immediately with cool water. Do not use ice.
2. Rinse the area and bandage.

For a severe burn, or if your dog is burned over a large part of his body:

1. Administer first aid for shock (see pages 154-155).
2. Get your dog to a veterinarian immediately.

Dehydration

There are two easy ways to check your dog for signs of dehydration.

1. Gently pinch the skin on your dog's back near the shoulder blades. The skin should gently snap back into place. If it slowly moves back into place, your dog may have mild dehydration. If it stays in a ridge, then your dog is seriously dehydrated.
2. Another way to check your dog for dehydration is to run your finger along his gum line. Your dog's gums should be moist and slippery. If they are dry or tacky, your dog may be dehydrated.

Avoid dehydration by giving your dog plenty of water. In very hot conditions, give your dog smaller amounts of water frequently. If your dog shows signs of severe dehydration, consult with a veterinarian immediately.

Diarrhea

Your dog can have diarrhea for any number of reasons. The cause may be simple, allowing for easy treatment, or very serious. You need to control the symptoms of diarrhea until you can have your dog checked by a veterinarian.

If your dog is not also vomiting, you may want to give him an antidiarrheal medication. Talk with your veterinarian about proper dosage for your dog *before* you leave on your camping trip. Watch for signs of dehydration. If your dog is not vomiting, give him small amounts of water often to prevent dehydration. If you are unsure of the cause, or if your dog has severe diarrhea, consult with a veterinarian as soon as possible. Diarrhea can be a symptom of a more serious illness.

Drowning

Most dogs will swim instinctively, but some dogs cannot swim. Even good swimmers, if unable to escape from the water, can become exhausted and drown. If your dog has drowned, he will not be breathing and you will need to take immediate steps to help him start breathing again.

1. Check your dog's throat to make sure that an object or the dog's tongue is not blocking the airway.
2. Hold your dog upside down by placing your arms around your dog's abdomen. Hold him upside down for about five seconds to drain the water out of his lungs.
3. Place your dog on his side and again check for an open airway and breathing. If your dog is not breathing, begin CPR (see pages 151-153). If your dog has started breathing, check for shock (see pages 154-155).

Dry, Sore, or Torn Pads

For dry or sore pads, use an ointment such as Bag Balm to soothe the pain. Give your dog a chance to rest his feet.

For torn pads:

1. If the tears are minor, treat as you would any other cut by cleaning the wound and using an antibiotic ointment.

2. Protect the torn pads with dog boots until they can be treated by a veterinarian.
3. If dog boots are not available, wrap the paws with cloth, gauze, or clean socks. Use adhesive tape to secure the wrapping.
4. Do not let your dog walk long distances until his pads heal.
5. Watch for infection.
6. See a veterinarian if the wounds are deep or if you have trouble keeping them clean.

Frostbite

The symptoms of frostbite include pale or red skin that is sensitive to the touch. The skin may blister and later may turn dark. To treat frostbite:

1. Warm up the area carefully using warm (not hot) water.
2. Rinse the area and loosely bandage it.
3. Have a veterinarian check the frostbitten area if there is skin damage. The damaged skin may need to be removed.
4. Watch for signs of shock (see pages 154-155).

Heatstroke

Signs of heatstroke include panting, weakness, vomiting, and diarrhea. The best treatment for heatstroke is prevention. Watch for signs of your dog becoming overheated, and take steps to cool him down immediately. To cool your dog down:

1. Have your dog lie down in a cool, shady spot.
2. Wet your dog down. You can do this by covering your dog with a wet towel. If you are near a water source, you may want to put your dog into the water for a few minutes. (Do not ice your dog, and do not submerge your dog in a snowmelt stream or other very cold water source—this could throw your dog into shock.) Use caution when cooling your dog off; it is very easy to overcool the dog, sending him into hypothermia.
3. If you have a thermometer, check your dog's temperature every few minutes. Stop the cooling process when his temperature reaches 104°F.

4. Encourage your dog to drink, but do not force water. Check for signs of dehydration (see page 158).
5. Check for signs of shock (see pages 154-155).
6. Consult with a veterinarian as soon as possible.

Hypothermia

Hypothermia is when the body's temperature falls below normal due to cold, wet, or windy conditions. The symptoms of hypothermia include shivering, confusion or disorientation, and signs of shock; in the late stages, your dog could lose consciousness. The best treatment for hypothermia is prevention. If your dog appears cold or is shivering, take immediate steps to warm him.

1. If the dog is wet, dry him off as much as possible.
2. Get him out of the wind and into a warm area.
3. Wrap him in a blanket or sleeping bag.
4. If your dog is conscious and is not vomiting, give him warm water or broth. Staying hydrated helps prevent hypothermia.
5. If he is still cold or has other symptoms of hypothermia, put him inside a sleeping bag with you. Your body heat will help warm him. You can put a smaller dog inside your jacket next to your body.
6. If you have a thermometer, check your dog's temperature every few minutes until his body temperature reaches 101°F.
7. Administer first aid for shock if necessary (see pages 154-155).
8. If your dog has signs of severe hypothermia, see a veterinarian as soon as possible.

Plant Poisoning

If your dog has eaten a wild mushroom or other poisonous plant:

1. Induce vomiting with hydrogen peroxide if your dog has just ingested the plant.
2. Administer first aid for shock (see pages 154-155).
3. Get your dog to a veterinarian immediately.
4. Identify the plant or bring a piece of it with you to help the veterinarian identify it.

Snakebite

If your dog has been bitten by a poisonous snake, you need to act quickly. He may have any of the following symptoms: an obvious bite showing two fang marks; pain, swelling, or redness; vomiting; difficulty in breathing; and signs of shock. (If your dog has been bitten by a nonpoisonous snake, the wound will appear more like a scratch and will not cause much swelling, redness, or pain.)

1. Get your dog to a veterinarian immediately. With immediate attention, most snakebites are treatable.
2. Keep your dog as still as possible. Carry your dog rather than letting him walk. This will slow the spread of the venom.
3. If you saw the snake, make note of any markings to help identify it. The veterinarian will need this information for the antivenin.
4. Do not wash the wound. Do not try to suck out the venom. Do not apply a tourniquet.
5. If the bite is on the foot or tail, apply a wide, flat, snug (not tight) bandage well above the wound to slow the spread of the venom. If the bite is on the leg, splint it to keep the leg still.
6. If you cannot get to a veterinarian right away, you may want to use a snakebite kit on your dog. Follow the directions on the kit.

Spider, Scorpion, or Ant Bites

If your dog has been bitten by a black widow spider or a scorpion, or if he has multiple bites from ants, he may experience pain, convulsions, fever, difficulty breathing, vomiting, and shock. Try to identify the source of the bite. Check your dog for shock (see pages 154-155). Get him to a veterinarian as soon as possible.

Toad Poisoning

Symptoms will vary for toad poisoning depending on the type of toad and the amount of venom that the dog ingested. Signs will include rubbing of the mouth, shaking of the head, vomiting, and shock. Flush your dog's mouth with water to get rid of any remaining poison, then treat your dog for shock (see pages 154-155). Get him to a veterinarian as soon as possible.

Torn Toenail

Torn toenails are very common when hiking.

1. Do not try to remove the toenail. Trim the end if needed.
2. Stop any bleeding from the nail using a styptic powder (Kwik Stop). Use pressure to stop bleeding in the surrounding area.
3. Clean the wound. Wrap it for protection or cover it with a dog boot.
4. Have a veterinarian check the nail to see if it will need to be removed.

Wild Animal Bites

If your dog is bitten by a wild animal, the type of treatment will depend somewhat on the severity of the bite.

For a minor bite:

1. Clip the dog's hair around the bite and clean the wound. Apply a loose bandage with an antibiotic ointment.
2. Watch for signs of infection.
3. Call your veterinarian to see if your dog should be seen for possible exposure to diseases carried by the wild animal.

For a deep bite, or for a dog that has multiple bites:

1. Control bleeding as needed.
2. Watch for signs of shock and treat shock as needed.
3. Clean and bandage the wounds.
4. Have your dog checked by a veterinarian as soon as possible.

Paw Note: *Make sure that your dog is vaccinated for rabies. If your dog is bitten by a wild animal, you will need to watch for signs of rabies, even if he has been vaccinated. The vaccination is not always 100 percent effective. Signs of rabies are a sudden change in behavior, restlessness, viciousness, drooling, and convulsions. If your dog exhibits any of these signs, get him to a veterinarian right away. If he has been bitten by a wild animal, take him for a rabies booster as soon as possible—even if it is not due.*

LEAVE ONLY PAW PRINTS

Camping with dogs has become an endangered activity. More and more areas are being closed to dogs, and the areas where you can still take dogs have stricter and stricter regulations. Some of the reasons are obvious. Wilderness areas are shrinking, the population of people and dogs is growing, and the places where the two meet have become more and more congested. Some trails that used to be quiet places of solitude and unhindered exploration have become akin to the Los Angeles freeway system. And where you have congestion, you have problems. Where there are problems, people come up with rules. Where there are rules, the rules get broken. When the rules get broken, you have more problems. If dogs are blamed for breaking those rules—well, you get the idea.

While we have brought up many things to think about and consider in this book, especially regarding responsibility, we want to emphasize that our goal is to encourage you to take the time to get to know your dog, yourself, and your natural surroundings.

Over the years, we have had the opportunity to travel and camp in a lot of different ways. We have taken our dogs on different types of adventures. Traveling with Charlie always reminded me that the wilderness was a great adventure, and that a dog's company could keep me feeling safe. Moose more than once gave me pause to recognize the great independent spirit of dogs. Cowboy accompanied me down paths that I was afraid to travel. Dakota will forever remind us that very real dangers lurk where you least suspect. Jesse keeps Melanee linked to her wild forbears and constantly reminds her that without pack (family) structure, we are lost. Blue keeps both of us having fun and living for today.

Perhaps the one common thread that has come from our variety of experiences with dogs and the wilderness is the need to tread lightly on the land—to respect the wild areas as if they were the most expensive and fragile crystal that could be easily broken. Unfortunately, as with fragile crystal, once our wilderness areas are damaged, they may never be restored. It is our responsibility, and we hope everyone's desire, to preserve the wilderness for future generations. When you camp, keep in mind the goal of saving the earth for future visits: by you, your kids, your grandkids—and their dogs!

What can you do? First, remember to always respect wildlife, and help your dog do the same. Second, try to have as little impact on an area as possible. Pack out your trash. Try not to disrupt plants and other natural features. Use care not to pollute water sources. Third, follow posted guidelines. Yes—those rules really are there for a reason. Breaking them may impact the natural balance and give power to those who want to limit access for dogs.

Always try to leave an area as you found it. You've heard the saying, "Take only memories, leave only footprints." Make that your camping motto. Only let's add, "Take only memories, leave only paw prints."

Happy camping to you and your canine companion!

APPENDIX A

NATIONAL FORESTS

USDA Forest Service
U.S. Department of Agriculture
P.O. Box 96090
Washington, D.C. 20090-6090
(202) 205-1760
http://www.fs.fed.us

Alaska Regional Office
Forest Service Information Center
709 W. 9th St.
Juneau, AK 99802-1628
(907) 586-8863

Eastern Regional Office
U.S. Forest Service
310 W. Wisconsin Ave., Room 500
Milwaukee, WI 53203
(414) 297-3693
(Illinois, Indiana, Iowa, Maine, Maryland, Massachusetts, Michigan, Minnesota, Missouri, New Hampshire, New Jersey, New York, Ohio, Pennsylvania, Rhode Island, Vermont, West Virginia, Wisconsin)

Intermountain Regional Office
U.S. Forest Service
Federal Bldg.
324 25th St.
Ogden, UT 84401-2301
(801) 625-5352
(Idaho, Nevada, Utah, Wyoming)

Northern Regional Office
U.S. Forest Service
Federal Bldg.
P.O. Box 7669
Missoula, MT 59807-7669
(406) 329-3511
(Idaho, Montana, North Dakota, South Dakota)

Pacific Northwest Regional Office
U.S. Forest Service
333 S.W. 1st Ave.
P.O. Box 3623
Portland, OR 97208
(503) 808-2636
(Oregon, Washington)

Pacific Southwest Regional Office
U.S. Forest Service
630 Sansome St.
San Francisco, CA 94111
(415) 705-2874
(California, Hawaii, Guam and Pacific Island Territories)

Rocky Mountain Regional Office
U.S. Forest Service
740 Simms St.
P.O. Box 25127
Lakewood, CO 80225
(303) 275-5350
(Colorado, Kansas, Nebraska, South Dakota, Wyoming)

Southern Regional Office
U.S. Forest Service
1720 Peachtree Rd., N.W.
Atlanta, GA 30367
(404) 347-2384
(Alabama, Arkansas, Florida, Georgia, Kentucky, Louisiana, Texas, Mississippi, North Carolina, Oklahoma, South Carolina, Puerto Rico, Tennessee, Virginia)

Southwestern Regional Office
U.S. Forest Service
Federal Building
517 Gold Ave., S.W.
Albuquerque, NM 87102
(505) 842-3292
(Arizona, New Mexico)

NATIONAL PARKS

National Park Service
1849 C St. N.W.
Washington, D.C. 20240
(202) 208-6843 Public Affairs
http://www.nps.gov

Alaska Field Area
National Park Service
2525 Gambell St., Rm. 107
Anchorage, AK 99503-2892
(907) 257-2687
(Alaska)

Intermountain Field Area
National Park Service
P.O. Box 25287
Denver, CO 80225-0287
(303) 969-2500
(Arizona, Colorado, Montana, New Mexico, Oklahoma, Texas, Utah, Wyoming)

Midwest Field Area
National Park Service
1709 Jackson St.
Omaha, NE 68102
(402) 221-3431
(Arkansas, Illinois, Indiana, Iowa, Kansas, Michigan, Minnesota, Missouri, Nebraska, North Dakota, Ohio, South Dakota, Wisconsin)

National Capital Field Area
National Park Service
1100 Ohio Dr., S.W.
Washington, D.C. 20242
(202) 619-7005
(Washington, D.C., with some units in Maryland, Virginia, West Virginia)

Northeast Field Area
National Park Service
200 Chestnut St., Room 306
Philadelphia, PA 19106
(215) 597-7013
(Connecticut, Delaware, Maine, Maryland, Massachusetts, New Hampshire, New Jersey, New York, Pennsylvania, Rhode Island, Vermont, Virginia, West Virginia)

Pacific West Field Area
National Park Service
600 Harrison St., Suite 600
San Francisco, CA 94107-1372
(415) 427-1304
(California, Hawaii, Idaho, Nevada, Oregon, Washington)

Southeast Field Area
National Park Service
1924 Bldg.
100 Alabama St., S.W.
Atlanta, GA 30303
(404) 331-5711
(Alabama, Georgia, Florida, Kentucky, Louisiana, Mississippi, North Carolina, South Carolina, Tennessee)

BUREAU OF LAND MANAGEMENT (BLM)

Office of Public Affairs
Rm. 750-LS, WO-530
1849 C St., N.W.
Washington, D.C. 20240
(202) 452-5125
http://www.blm.gov

Alaska State Office
Bureau of Land Management
222 W. 7th Ave., Rm. 13
Anchorage, AK 99513
(907) 271-5960
(Alaska)

Arizona State Office
Bureau of Land Management
222 N. Central Ave.
Phoenix, AZ 85004-2203
(602) 417-9200
(Arizona)

California State Office
Bureau of Land Management
2135 Butano Dr.
Sacramento, CA 95825
(916) 978-4400
(California)

Colorado State Office
Bureau of Land Management
2850 Youngfield St.
Lakewood, CO 80215-7093
(303) 239-3600
(Colorado, Kansas)

Eastern States Office
Bureau of Land Management
7450 Boston Blvd.
Springfield, VA 22153
(703) 440-1600
(Arkansas, Iowa, Louisiana, Missouri, Minnesota, and all states east of
the Mississippi)

Idaho State Office
Visitor Center
1387 S. Vinnell Way
Boise, ID 83709-1657
(208) 373-4007
(Idaho)

Montana and Dakotas State Office
Bureau of Land Management
222 N. 32nd St.
P.O. Box 36800
Billings, MT 59107-6800
(406) 255-2885
(Montana, North Dakota, South Dakota)

Nevada State Office
Bureau of Land Management
850 Harvard Way
P.O. Box 12000
Reno, NV 89520-0006
(702) 861-6500
(Nevada)

New Mexico State Office
Bureau of Land Management
P.O. Box 27115
Santa Fe, NM 87502-0115
(505) 438-7400
(New Mexico, Oklahoma, Texas, Kansas)

Oregon State Office
Bureau of Land Management
P.O. Box 2965
Portland, OR 97208-2965
(503) 952-6001
(Oregon, Washington)

Utah State Office
Bureau of Land Management
P.O. Box 45155
Salt Lake City, UT 84145-0155
(801) 539-4001
(Utah)

Wyoming State Office
Bureau of Land Management
5353 Yellowstone
P.O. Box 1828
Cheyenne, WY 82003
(307) 775-6256
(Nebraska, Wyoming)

STATE PARKS

Alabama Department of Conservation and Natural Resources
Division of State Parks
64 N. Union St.
Montgomery, AL 36130
(800) 252-7275 (ALA-PARK)

Alaska State Parks
Public Information Center
3601 C St., Suite 200
Anchorage, AK 99503-5929
(907) 269-8400

Arizona State Parks
1300 W. Washington, Suite 104
Phoenix, AZ 85007
(602) 542-4174

Arkansas Department of Parks and Tourism
One Capitol Mall
Little Rock, AR 72201
(501) 682-1191

California State Parks
Office of Public Relations
P.O. Box 942896
Sacramento, CA 94296-0001
(916) 653-6995

Colorado Division of Parks and Outdoor Recreation
1313 Sherman St., Rm. 618
Denver, CO 80203
(303) 866-3437

Connecticut Department of Environmental Protection
State Parks Division
79 Elm St.
Hartford, CT 06106-5127
(860) 424-3200

Delaware Department of Natural Resources and Environmental Control
Division of Parks and Recreation
89 Kings Hwy.
P.O. Box 1401
Dover, DE 19903
(302) 739-4702

Florida Department of Environmental Protection
Division of Recreation and Parks
3900 Commonwealth Blvd.
Mail Station 535
Tallahassee, FL 32399-3000
(805) 488-9872

Georgia Parks and Historic Sites Division
Department of Natural Resources
Floyd Tower East, Suite 1352
205 Butler St., S.E.
Atlanta, GA 30334
(404) 656-3530
(800) 869-8420

Hawaii Department of Land and Natural Resources
Division of State Parks
P.O. Box 621
Honolulu, HI 96809
(808) 587-0300

Idaho Department of Parks and Recreation
P.O. Box 83720
Boise, ID 83720-0065
(208) 334-4199

Illinois Department of Natural Resources
524 S. 2nd St., Rm. 500
Springfield, IL 62701-1787
(217) 782-7454

Indiana Department of Natural Resources
Division of State Parks and Reservoirs
402 W. Washington St., Rm. W298
Indianapolis, IN 46204
(317) 232-4124

Iowa Department of Natural Resources
Wallace State Office Bldg.
502 E. 9th St.
Des Moines, IA 50319
(515) 281-5198

Kansas Department of Wildlife and Parks
512 S.E. 25th Ave.
Pratt, KS 67124
(316) 672-5911

Kentucky Department of Parks
500 Mero St., CPT 10th Floor
Frankfort, KY 40601
(502) 564-2172
(800) 255-PARK

Louisiana Department of Culture, Recreation, and Tourism
Office of State Parks
P.O. Box 44426
Baton Rouge, LA 70804
(504) 342-8111

Maine Bureau of Parks and Land
Department of Conservation
State House Station 22
Augusta, ME 04333-0022
(207) 287-3821

Maryland Department of Natural Resources
State Forest and Park Service
Tawes State Office Bldg.
580 Taylor Ave. E3
Annapolis, MD 21401
(410) 260-8168

Massachusetts Department of Environmental Management
Division of Forests and Parks
100 Cambridge St., 19th Floor
Boston, MA 02202
(617) 727-3180

Michigan Department of Natural Resources
Parks Division
P.O. Box 30257
Lansing, MI 48909
(517) 373-1270

Minnesota Department of Natural Resources
Division of Parks and Recreation
500 Lafayette Rd.
St. Paul, MN 55155-4040
(612) 296-6157

Mississippi Department of Wildlife, Fisheries, and Parks
Office of Parks
P.O. Box 451
Jackson, MS 39205-0451
(800) GO-PARKS (467-2757)

Missouri Department of Natural Resources
Division of State Parks
P.O. Box 176
Jefferson City, MO 65102
(573) 751-2479
(800) 334-6946

Montana Department of Fish, Wildlife, and Parks
Park Division
P.O. Box 200701
Helena, MT 59620-0701
(406) 444-3750

Nebraska Game and Parks Commission
2200 N. 33rd St.
P.O. Box 30370
Lincoln, NE 68503
(402) 471-0641

Nevada Department of Conservation and Natural Resources
Division of State Parks
1300 S. Curry St.
Carson City, NV 89703
(702) 687-4384

New Hampshire Division of Parks and Recreation
P.O. Box 1856
Concord, NH 03302
(603) 271-3556

New Jersey Department of Environmental Protection
Division of Parks and Forestry
State Park Service
P.O. Box 404
501 E. State St.
Trenton, NJ 08625
(609) 984-0370
(800) 843-6420

New Mexico Natural Resources Department
State Parks and Recreation Division
2040 S. Pacheco
P.O. Box 1147
Santa Fe, NM 87505
(505) 827-7173

New York Office of Parks, Recreation, and Historic Preservation
Empire State Plaza, Bldg. 1
Albany, NY 12223
(518) 474-0456

North Carolina Department of Environment and Natural Resources
Division of Parks and Recreation
P.O. Box 27687
Raleigh, NC 27611
(919) 733-4181

North Dakota Parks and Recreation Department
1835 E. Bismark Expressway
Bismark, ND 58504
(701) 328-5357

Ohio Department of Natural Resources
Division of Parks and Recreation
1952 Belcher Dr., Bldg. C3
Columbus, OH 43224
(614) 265-6561

Oklahoma Division of State Parks
P.O. Box 52002
Oklahoma City, OK 73152
(405) 521-3411

Oregon State Parks
1115 Commercial St., N.E.
Salem, OR 97310
(503) 378-6305
(800) 551-6949

Pennsylvania Bureau of State Parks
P.O. Box 8551
Harrisburg, PA 17105-8551
(800) 63-PARKS (637-2757)

Rhode Island Department of Environmental Management
Division of Parks and Recreation
2321 Hartford Ave.
Johnston, RI 02919
(401) 222-2635

South Carolina State Parks
1205 Pendleton St.
Columbia, SC 29201
(803) 734-0156

South Dakota Department of Game, Fish, and Parks
Division of Parks and Recreation
Joe Foss Bldg.
523 E. Capitol Ave.
Pierre, SD 57501-3182
(605) 773-3391

Tennessee Bureau of State Parks
Department of Environment and Conservation
401 Church St., 7th Floor
Nashville, TN 37243
(615) 532-0001

Texas Parks and Wildlife Department
4200 Smith School Rd.
Austin, TX 78744
(800) 792-1112

Utah Division of Parks and Recreation
Administrative Office
1594 W. North Temple, Suite 116
P.O. Box 146001
Salt Lake City, UT 84114-6001
(801) 538-7220

Vermont Agency of Natural Resources
Department of Forests, Parks, and Recreation
103 S. Main St., 10 South
Waterbury, VT 05671
(802) 241-3655

Virginia Department of Conservation and Recreation
Division of State Parks
203 Governor St., Suite 302
Richmond, VA 23219
(804) 786-1712

Washington State Parks and Recreation Commission
7150 Cleanwater Lane
P.O. Box 42650
Olympia, WA 98504
(800) 233-0321

West Virginia Division of Natural Resources
Parks and Recreation
State Capitol Complex
Bldg. 3, Room 714
Charleston, WV 25305-0662
(304) 558-2764

Wisconsin Department of Natural Resources
Bureau of Parks and Recreation
Box 7921
Madison, WI 53707-7921
(608) 266-2181

Wyoming Division of State Parks and Historic Sites
1st Floor, Herschler Bldg.
Cheyenne, WY 82002
(307) 777-3680

DOG CAMPS

Camp Gone to the Dogs
Putney, VT 05346
(802) 387-5673
Director: Honey Loring

Dog Days of Wisconsin
1879 Haymarket #24
Waukesha, WI 53186
(800) 226-7436
Director: Pamela J. Paulson

Lake Tahoe's Camp Winnaribbun
P.O. Box 50300
Reno, NV 89513
(702) 747-1561
Director: Lory Kohlmoos

Legacy Camp
P.O. Box 3909
Sequim, WA 98382
(360) 683-1522
Director: Terry Ryan

Wiz Kid Dog Camp
4 Brookside Place
Westport, CT 06880
(203) 226-9556
Director: Cynthia Gillette Fox, Ph.D.

GUIDEBOOKS

General

America's Secret Recreation Areas—Your Recreation Guide to the Bureau of Land Management's Wild Lands of the West
by Michael Hodgson
Foghorn Press
555 DeHaro St., Suite 220
San Francisco, CA 94107

Foghorn Outdoors: America's Wilderness
by Buck Tilton
Foghorn Press
555 DeHaro St., Suite 220
San Francisco, CA 94107
Foghorn also publishes campground guides for California, the Pacific Northwest, and the Rocky Mountains. These books are well organized and are particularly helpful for beginning campers. They also list where dogs are permitted.

Hidden Rockies—The Adventurer's Guide
by John Gottberg and Richard Harris
Ulysses Press
P.O. Box 3440
3286 Adeline St., Suite 1
Berkeley, CA 94703-3440

The Adventurer's Guide is a series that covers many regions of the United States. In addition to campgrounds, these guides offer information on restaurants, shops, nightlife, hikes, and things to do such as fishing and biking. They let you know where dogs are permitted and give helpful warnings about indigenous wildlife.

Parks Directory of the United States, 2nd edition
Darren L. Smith, editor
Omnigraphics, Inc.
Penobscot Bldg.
Detroit, MI 48226
An extremely comprehensive guide to national parks, national forests, state parks, BLM land, and nearly any other U.S. administered national- and state-park agency. Although this book can be ordered through a local bookstore, it is available in most library reference sections.

Recreation Lakes of California
by D. J. Dirksen
Recreation Sales Publishing
P.O. Box 1028
Aptos, CA 95001
Provides a list of recreational sites throughout California and the facilities available at each. Has a section addressing the rules regarding pets at most sites.

Trailer Life Campground/RV Park and Service Directory
Joe Daquino, Publisher
2575 Vista Del Mar Dr.
Ventura, CA 93001-2575
Provides a comprehensive list of campgrounds for motor homes, travel trailers, fifth wheels, and campers. Indicates where dogs are permitted.

Woodall's Camping Frontier West
Woodall Publications Corporation
13975 West Polo Trail Dr.
Lake Forest, IL 60045-5000
Woodall also publishes a *'96 Eastern Campground Directory*. Both give information regarding where dogs are permitted.

Dog-Specific

DogGone Newsletter
Wendy Ballard
P.O. Box 651155
Vero Beach, FL 36965
This is not actually a book, but a bimonthly newsletter that highlights pet-friendly destinations across the United States and travel tips for people who vacation with their dogs. They also have database search service for subscribers that includes more than 23,000 accommodations for people traveling with dogs, including campgrounds and RV parks. A great resource!

The California Dog Lover's Companion
by Maria Goodavage
Foghorn Press
555 DeHaro St., Suite 220
San Francisco, CA 94107
An extensive list of lodgings, restaurants, campgrounds, parks, hikes, and other fun activities for you and your dog. Foghorn Press has also published the *Seattle* and the *Florida Dog Lover's Companion*.

Eileen's Directory of . . . series
by Eileen Barish
Pet-Friendly Publications
P.O. Box 8459
Scottsdale, AZ 85252
An informative guide to hotels, restaurants, activities, parks and trails for you and your dog. Does not list camping areas. The series includes California and Arizona.

Frommer's On the Road Again with Man's Best Friend, 3rd edition
by Dawn and Robert Habgood
Howell Book House
1633 Broadway
New York, NY 10019
This book is one in a series that spans the Northwest, Midatlantic, New England, California, and the Southeast. General travel rather than camping-specific.

APPENDIX G

OUR FAVORITE CAMPING, TRAINING, AND DOG BOOKS

Dog Camping and Hiking

Backpacking with Your Dog
by Richard Lerner, DVM
Menasha Ridge Press
3169 Cahaba Heights
Birmingham, AL 35243

Favorite Dog Hikes in and around Los Angeles
by Wynne Benti
Spotted Dog Press
P.O. Box CF
Tujunga, CA 91403-0736

A Guide to Backpacking with Your Dog
by Charlene G. LaBelle
Alpine Publications
P.O. Box 7027
Loveland, CO 80537

On the Trail with Your Canine Companion
by Cheryl S. Smith
Howell Book House
1633 Broadway
New York, NY 10019

General Camping

The Camper's and Backpacker's Bible
by Tom Huggler
Doubleday
1540 Broadway
New York, NY 10036

The Camper's Companion
by Rick Greenspan and Hal Kahn
Publishing Manager
Foghorn Press
555 De Haro St., Suite 220
San Francisco, CA 94107
(This is our favorite camping book!)

*The Complete Idiot's Guide to Hiking, Camping
and the Great Outdoors*
by Michael Mouland
Alpha Books
1633 Broadway
New York, NY 10019

The Complete Walker III, 3rd revision
by Colin Fletcher
Alfred A. Knopf
Available in most bookstores.

Kayak Camping
by David Harrison
Hearst Marine Books
1350 Avenue of the Americas
New York, NY 10019

Kids Outdoors
by Victoria and Frank Logue and Mark Carroll
Ragged Mountain Press
Customer Service Department
P.O. Box 547
Blacklick, OH 43004

The Sierra Club Family Outdoors Guide
by Marilyn Doan
Sierra Club
Department J-918, P.O. Box 7959
San Francisco, CA 94120

Dog-Training Books

The Canine Good Citizen
by Jack and Wendy Volhard
Howell Book House
15 Columbus Circle
New York, NY 10023

Don't Shoot the Dog
by Karen Pryor
Bantam Books
1540 Broadway
New York, NY 10036

Enjoying Dog Agility from Backyard to Competition
by Julie Daniels
Doral Publishing
Available through: Dog and Cat Book Catalog
Direct Book Service
P.O. Box 2778
Wenatchee, WA 98807-2778

How to Raise A Puppy You Can Live With
by Clarice Rutherford and David H. Neil, MRCVS
Alpine Publications
P.O. Box 7027
Loveland, CO 80537

How to Talk to Your Dog
by Jean Craighead George
Warner Books, Inc.
666 5th Ave.
New York, NY 10103

Owner's Guide to Better Behavior in Dogs
by William E. Campbell
Alpine Publications
P.O. Box 7027
Loveland, CO 80537

First Aid for Dogs

Emergency First Aid for Your Dog
by Tamara S. Shearer, DVM
Ohio Distinctive Publishing
4588 Kenny Rd.
Columbus, OH 43220

First Aid for Dogs and Cats
by Jean Allbright, DVM
Type-Com, Inc.
1605 W. University, Suite 109
Tempe, AZ 85281

Help! The Quick Guide to First Aid for Your Dog
by Michelle Bamberger, DVM
Howell Book House
866 3rd Ave.
New York, NY 10022

Homeopathy: First Aid for Pets
Day (UK), 1992
Available through: Dog and Cat Book Catalog
Direct Book Service
P.O. Box 2778
Wenatchee, WA 98807-2778

Pet First Aid
by Bobbie Mammato, DVM, MPH
Mosby-Year Book, Inc.
11830 Westline Industrial Dr.
St. Louis, MO 63146
Available through your local American Red Cross
(Great book! Developed through the combined effort of the American
Red Cross and The Humane Society of the United States.)

DOG GEAR AND SUPPLIES

General Dog Supplies

Doctor's Foster and Smith
2253 Air Park Rd.
P.O. Box 100
Rhinelander, WI 54501-0100
(800) 826-7206 Phone
(800) 776-8872 Fax
Catalog selection includes beds, toys, backpacks, The Springer, crates, and many sweaters and jackets. No minimum order is required.

J. B. Wholesale Pet Supplies, Inc.
5 Raritan Rd.
Oakland, NJ 07436
(800) 526-0388
Catalog selection includes ponchos, sweaters, and jackets as well as crates, beds, leashes, backpacks, and flea- and tick-control devices. Minimum order of $25 is required.

Pet Warehouse
Department C46D
P.O. Box 310
Xenia, OH 45385
(800) 443-1160 Phone
(800) 513-1913 Fax

Catalog offers a variety of beds, reflector collars, life vests, toys, and flea- and tick-control products. No minimum order is required.

R. C. Steele
1989 Transit Way, Box 910
Brockport, NY 14420-0910
(800) 872-3773
Catalog contains a variety of products for your dog, including crates, The Springer, life preservers, grooming supplies, tie outs, and toys. Minimum order of $50 required.

Packing, Sledding, and Other Gear

DogStuf
231 Rubie Crescent
P.O. Box 509
Nobleford, Alberta, Canada
(403) 824-3300
A variety of dog packs for activities, including a weekend hike, a camping getaway or a backpacking adventure. Also carries a portable water dish.

Ikon Outfitters, Ltd.
7597 Latham Rd.
Lodi, WI 53555
(608) 592-4397
Sleds, skijoring tow bars, multipurpose harnesses, packs, and boots are provided in this catalog.

Nordkyn Outfitters
P.O. Box 1023
Graham, WA 98338-1023
(253) 847-4128
Offers many packs, ganglines, sleds, boots, skijoring equipment and harnesses.

Wenaha Dog Packs
4518 Maltby Rd.
Bothell, WA 98012
(800) 917-0707
(206) 488-2397
Offers a selection of packs, including a sled pack, with an excellent range of sizes.

Wolf Packs
755 Tyler Creek Rd.
Ashland, OR 97520-9408
(541) 482-SNOW (482-7669)
Includes packs, water bowls, toys, books, collars, and leashes.

Specialized Gear for Your Dog

Pée Dee's Paw Protectors
7416 Altiva Place
Carlsbad, CA 92009
(760) 438-8226
Dog boots made from neoprene with the bottom reinforced with 1000
dyner Cordura. The boots fasten with Velcro for an easy fit. They are
designed to protect your dog's paws from snow, heat, gravel, and other
potentially harmful conditions. Fit sizes extra small to giant.

Best Buddy Food and Water Bowl
Raving Artists Designs
P.O. Box 122
Copper Center, AK 99573
(907) 822-5487 Phone/Fax
A collapsible combination of pack cloth and rip-stop nylon. This water
bowl holds two quarts of food or water and is compact and durable.

Classic Cover-Ups
9 Marie Lane
West Grove, PA 19390
(610) 869-3250
Blanket coats made of Gore-Tex, Cordura, or nylon and insulated with
Hollofil. Great protection in wet and cold weather, waterproof, available in a range of sizes and machine washable.

Body Cooler Products
8700 Commerce Park Dr., Ste. 212
Houston, TX 77036
Akemi, Inc.
(800) 209-2665
(713) 541-0318 Fax
Products designed to keep your dog cool. The special nontoxic crystals
contained in the selections of bandannas, belly wraps, and crate mats
stay cool for hours after being soaked in cold water.

Poocheroo
6578 McAbee Rd.
San Jose, CA 95120
(800) 622-3775
Holds dogs up to fifteen pounds. Made from denim with polypropylene
straps and side-clasp buckles. Dogs fit entirely inside.

Pet Pouch
P.O. Box 797144
Dallas, TX 75379
(972) 931-6534
Carries small dogs by supporting their torsos while allowing
their arms and legs to dangle freely.

Pet Pak, Inc.
P.O. Box 982
Edison, NJ 08818-0982
(800) 217-PETS (217-7387)
http://www.pet-pak.com
Includes a first-aid guide, bandages, and treatments for cuts, burns,
insect bites, ticks, and more. The kits come in different sizes. Larger
kits contain a greater variety of products.

The Springer
Available through Drs. Foster and Smith and R. C. Steele catalogs.
This device attaches to the frame of your bicycle and your dog's leash
attaches to it. The Springer enables you to maintain your balance
even when your dog is straining at his leash by absorbing the impact
with a spring.

K9 Cruiser Bicycle Leash
4640 De Soto St.
San Diego, CA 92109
(800) K9-CRUISE (592-7847)
The special design of the K9 Cruiser and the location of the attach-
ment to your bike help counterbalance any tugging your dog might do
on his leash while running alongside you.

CycleTote Corp.
517 N. Link Ln.
Ft. Collins, CO 80524
(800) 747-2407
CycleTote makes bike trailers specifically designed for dogs.

GEAR AND EQUIPMENT FOR PEOPLE

Boundary Waters Catalog
Piragis Northwoods Co.
105 N. Central Ave.
Ely, MN 55731
(800) 223-6565
A selection of canoes, packs, cold-weather gear, and supplies, including trail foods and cooking gear. Fascinating selection of books. Also carries jewelry, at-home furniture, calendars, and more for the camper who loves to shop.

Campmor
P.O. Box 700-B4
Saddle River, NJ 07458-0700
(800) 525-4784
Carries equipment and clothing for most camping adventures on land. Also has biking equipment. Good prices.

L. L. Bean, Inc.
Freeport, ME 04033-0001
(800) 221-4221
Wide selection of camping gear and clothing. Products are of good quality and are priced accordingly.

Mountainsmith
18301 W. Colfax Ave.
Heritage Square Bldg. P
Golden, CO 80401
(800) 426-4075
A variety of backpacks for hiking, camping, rock and ice climbing. Also includes a style of pack for your dog.

Northwest River Supplies, Inc. (NRS)
2009 S. Main St.
Moscow, ID 83843-8913
(800) 635-5202
A catalog filled with kayaks, canoes, inflatable boats and supplies. Includes rescue equipment, clothing, repair kits, and life jackets. Also carries life vests for your dog.

REI Catalog
1700 45th St., East
Sumner, WA 98352
(800) 426-4840
REI (Recreational Equipment, Inc.) is a cooperative with good prices and an excellent selection of camping gear and clothing.

APPENDIX J

DOG, CAMPING, AND TRAVEL ORGANIZATIONS

American Kennel Club
5580 Centerview Dr..
Raleigh, NC 27606-3390

California Canine Hikers
2154 Woodlyn Rd.
Pasadena, CA 91104

Mixed Breed Dog Club of America
13884 State Route 104
Lucasville, OH 45648-8586

Sierra Club's K9 Committee
3345 Wilshire Blvd., #508
Los Angeles, CA 90010-1816

United Kennel Club
100 E. Kilgore Rd.
Kalamazoo, MI 49001-5598

American Canoe Association
7432 Alban Station Blvd., Suite B-226
Springfield, VA 22150

Camping Women
7623 Southbreeze Dr.
Sacramento, CA 95828

Canoe
131 East Murray St.
Fort Wayne, IN 46803

Family Campers and RVers
4804 Transit Rd., Bldg. 2
Depew, NY 14043

National Campers and Hikers Association
7172 Transit Rd.
Buffalo, NY 14221

North American Family Campers Association
16 Evergreen Terrace
North Reading, MA 01864

Sierra Club
85 2nd St., 2nd Floor
San Francisco, CA 94105

United States Canoe Association
9021 F. North 91st St.
Milwaukee, WI 53224

PERIODICALS

AKC Gazette
51 Madison Ave.
New York, NY 10010-1686

Dog Fancy
P.O. Box 6050
Irvine, CA 92718

Dog World
745 5th Ave.
New York, NY 10151

Good Dog!
P.O. Box 31292
Charleston, SC 29417-1292

North America Dog Magazine
Dogs International
P.O. Box 2270
Alpine, CA 91903-2270

Your Dog
P.O. Box 420272
Palm Coast, FL 32142-0272

Backpacker
Rodale Press, Inc.
33 E. Minor St.
Emmaus, PA 18098

Camping Today
4804 Transit Rd., Bldg. 2
Depew, NY 14043-4704

Canoe & Kayak
P.O. Box 7011
Red Oak, IA 51591-4011

Rodale's Guide to Family Camping
Family Camping Magazine
33 E. Minor St.
Emmaus, PA 18098-0099

Sierra
85 2nd St., 2nd Floor
San Francisco, CA 94105

THE COMPLETE CANINE
CAMPER CHECKLIST

We consider the items with a * to be absolute essentials. The other items should be taken along as appropriate for you and your dog.

- *Shelter (can share yours!)
- *Bedding
- *Food (enough for the trip plus three-day emergency supply)
- *Food and water bowl
- Treats
- *Regular medications (enough for trip plus a three-day emergency supply)
- *Flat collar with camping ID
- Training collar (if applicable)
- *Regular leash
- Long leash, tie out, or crate
- Dog sweater or parka (as needed, depending on conditions and dog)
- Dog pack
- Dog boots (may be included in first-aid supplies)
- *Plastic bags, pooper scooper or trowel
- *Dog towel
- *Brush and flea comb
- Soap or shampoo
- *Flea, tick and other insect repellents
- Sunscreen
- Life jacket (if traveling by boat)

- *Health certificate or proof of vacinations
- Canine Good Citizen certificate or obedience completion certificate
- Toys and chewies
- *First-aid kit

FIRST-AID KIT
- 2-inch roll gauze
- Nonstick gauze bandages
- Adhesive tape or vet wrap (also called sports wrap—sticks to itself, not fur)
- Tweezers (the type on a Swiss Army knife work well)
- Small scissors for clipping fur (get good scissors—they are worth the extra expense)
- Antibiotic ointment (Neosporin, bacitracin or calendula gel)
- Antiseptic wipes or soap (Betadine)
- Boots (if not already included with your gear)
- Hydrogen peroxide—3% solution (1 tbsp. for every 15-20 pounds, to induce vomiting. Repeat only once in ten minutes if no vomiting occurs. Please discuss proper dosage for your dog with your veterinarian.)

For a more complete kit add:
- Cortisone cream
- Bag Balm
- Thermometer (be sure to ask your veterinarian to show you how to take your dog's temperature)
- Snakebite kit
- Instant cold pack
- Ace bandage
- Nail clippers
- Styptic powder (Kwik Stop)

Medications you may also want to include (please talk with your veterinarian about using these medications in an emergency and the proper dosage for your dog):
- Anti-diarrheal (Loperamide or Kaopectate)
- Antihistamine (Benadryl)
- Aspirin (Only if your veterinarian recommends aspirin for your dog. *Never* give your dog Tylenol or ibuprofen.)

Add these additional items for people:
- Moleskins
- Regular bandages
- Anti-itch medication (Calamine or Caladryl)
- Lip balm

ABOUT THE AUTHORS

Mardi Richmond and Melanee L. Barash agree that camping with dogs is an ideal vacation. After all, what could be better than heading off into the wilderness with your best four-legged friend? Mardi started camping with dogs more than twenty years ago and has shared everything from weekend car camping to lengthy wilderness adventures with her canine companions. Melanee's adventures with camping began when she was a teenager. As a city girl new to the great outdoors, she was hooked from the start. And once she discovered camping with dogs, she realized that her dog had been the essential missing item from her original "what to pack" list.

When the authors are not spending time in the wilderness, Mardi is a writer and editor, specializing in the fields of health education and (you guessed it) dogs. She has had her articles published in *Dog Fancy*, *Dane World*, and other dog-related publications. Melanee is a psychotherapist who works with humans and who occasionally includes dogs in the healing process. She also worked at the Animal Fitness Center as a hydrotherapist for dogs. Today, Mardi and Melanee share their camping adventures with two terrific dogs, Jesse and Blue.

INDEX

ADDITIONAL TITLES OF INTEREST

Backpacking With Your Dog
Charlene LaBelle
A how-to book for the person who wants to teach a dog to carry a
backpack. Includes conditioning, weights a dog can be expected to
carry, types of dog packs, how to pack them, food to take,
and much more.

201 Ways to Enjoy Your Dog
Ellie Milon
No matter what breed you own or where your personal interests
lie, there are activities you can share with your canine companion.
This books talks about all the different organized activities
in North America.

Owner's Guide to Better Behavior in Dogs
William Campbell
Basic training, understanding your dog's behavior, communicating
with your canine, shaping behavior positively to avoid problems
later, and correcting problem behaviors are discussed.
Essential for every dog owner!

The Story of Scotch
Enos Mills, with supplemental chapters by Kent Dannen
A great book to read by the fire while camping!
Mills, the founder of Rocky Mountain National Park, loved and
learned from his Border Collie, Scotch, and he wrote passionately
about their mutual adventures. Dannen adds a modern-day
perspective, discussing the pleasure of taking a dog when hiking or
backpacking in wilderness areas.

FOR A CATALOG OF ALPINE BOOKS
Call 1-800-777-7257
Fax 970-667-9157
email Alpinecsr@aol.com
Write Alpine Publications, 225 S. Madison, Loveland, CO 80537